DIVIDED CITY

First published 1978
O'Brien Educational
11 Clare Street, Dublin 2, Ireland

ISBN 0 905140 50 8 (hardback)
ISBN 0 905140 51 6 (paperback)

Cover design: Jarlath Hayes
Binding: John F. Newman Ltd.
Typesetting: Redsetter Ltd.
Printed by E. & T. O'Brien Ltd.,
11 Clare Street, Dublin 2, Ireland.

BEV

DIVIDED CITY

Portrait of Dublin 1913

CURRICULUM DEVELOPMENT UNIT, DUBLIN

O'BRIEN

The Curriculum Development Unit

The Curriculum Development Unit was established in September 1972. It is sponsored by the City of Dublin Vocational Education Committee and works in co-operation with the School of Education in Trinity College, Dublin, with the approval of the Department of Education. It has a steering committee composed of representatives of these three bodies.

The Unit has concentrated on the curricular areas of Humanities, Science and Outdoor Education. The Unit Director is Anton Trant.

Humanities Co-ordinator: Tony Crooks
Humanities Team: Nora Godwin 1973 —
                                    Agnes McMahon 1975-76
                                    Bernard O'Flaherty 1976-

This collection has been researched and edited for publication by
Gary Granville

Prior to publication, the following schools were involved in the development, use and revision of the collection. The suggestions and comments of the teachers in these schools have been used as a basis for the edition.

Christian Brothers School, James's Street; Christian Brothers School, Parnell Road; Colaiste Dhulaigh, Coolock; Colaiste Eanna, Cabra; Colaiste Eoin, Finglas; Coolmine Community School, Clonsilla; Dominican Convent, Ballyfermot; Gonzaga College, Dublin; Holy Child School, Killiney; Liberties Vocational School, Dublin; Loreto Convent, Cavan; Mater Dei Secondary School, Basin Lane; Pobal Scoil Iosa, Malahide; Rosary College, Crumlin; St. Clare's Secondary School, Ballyjamesduff; Scoil Ide, Finglas; The Technical Institute, Ringsend; Vocational School, Ballyfermot; Vocational School, Cavan; Vocational School for Boys, Clogher Road; Vocational School, Crumlin Road; Vocational School, Dundrum; Vocational School, Lucan; Vocational School, Sallynoggin.

4

Contents

Irish Life, 19th September, 1913.

HE Gaiety Theatre was crowded—in spite of strikes and the absence of tram—last Monday night. The occasion was the first production of a farce called "Oh! I Say!!" (Three notes of exclamation altogether in the title.) This little dramatic trifle comes from the French. It was watered down to suit a London audience when it was first presented there last May. It has since undergone a further process of docking and cutting. And

we may meet with none of the mischances that befell Marcel Durosel, the bridegroom of the farce.

     ⊙   ⊙   ⊙

Marcel had been flighty in his bachelor days. He had flirted with an actress, Sidonie de Matine. And the Fates arranged a nice little punishment for him. He was doomed to spend his honeymoon in the flat of his former sweetheart, Sidonie. Sidonie was away on tour. And her maid wanted to earn an honest penny.

A bustling Earl Street at the corner of O'Connell Street. It is twenty minutes past two and the city is crowded with bargain-hunters at the sales. Bare feet and bowler hats are in evidence.

1
Dublin, Ireland and the Empire

I was tremendously proud of belonging to the Empire, as were at that
time most Irishmen. I gloried in all its trappings, Kings, Queens, dukes,
duchesses, generals, admirals, soldiers, sailors, colonists and conquerors, the
lot.   *Sean O'Faolain*

"LIFE IS GOOD here in Dublin" a British Army officer wrote to
his father in 1912. Captain Vane de Vallance, of the Fifth Royal
Irish Lancers, was newly arrived in Ireland and like anyone else in
his position he took a great interest in his new surroundings.
Although he did not know it when he came, he was to witness
many important events in Dublin over the next few years.

The British Army, of course, was no stranger to Ireland. Since
the Act of Union in 1800, this country had been part of the
United Kingdom of Great Britain and Ireland, ruled by the British
Government in London. The people of Ireland therefore shared
the same laws, and the same army, as the rest of the United
Kingdom. The overall Head of State was the King, but he
nominated a representative in Ireland: this person, the Viceroy or
Lord Lieutenant, had an official home in the Viceregal Lodge in
the Phoenix Park. However, he had no real power. The Viceroy
acted only on the advice of the Chief Secretary for Ireland, just
as the King himself was a figurehead; the responsibility for running
the country properly belonging to the Prime Minister and Government. The most powerful person in Ireland around 1913 was,
therefore, Augustine Birrell, the Chief Secretary. Birrell was an
Englishman, a well-known writer and a good administrator. From
his offices in Dublin Castle he supervised the day-to-day government of Ireland, and was in fact one of the most important public

figures in the entire United Kingdom.

Dublin was the main city of Ireland, but it was not a capital city in the usual sense of the word. Despite the fact that there was no Irish government in the city, many of the activities normally associated with a capital city were carried on. If you had been a member of the upper classes in Dublin in 1913, an invitation to the Viceregal Lodge would have been considered the highest honour, and it was sought after by many. The Viceroy and his wife, Lord and Lady Aberdeen, were reported in detail in all the fashionable society magazines, and were very popular. They took part in social events of all kinds, mainly parties and balls, but also took an interest in charity work, and encouraged other people to do so as well. The Chief Secretary, Augustine Birrell, however, was not so popular. Fashionable society considered him dull. But then he had far more serious problems to take up his time — it was a period of great uncertainty in Ireland, and the political problems of the day must have left him little time or inclination for parties.

IRISH POLITICS

Since its introduction, the Act of Union had been opposed by many people in Ireland. In the 1880s, Charles Stewart Parnell had succeeded in forming the 'Home Rule Party' with support from some of the Irish members of the London Parliament. By 'Home Rule' they meant the setting up of an Irish Parliament which would manage all the affairs of Ireland while still remaining part of the United Kingdom. Parnell died in 1891 but the Home Rule party carried on and by 1913, with John Redmond as its leader, it seemed as if they might at last succeed in forcing the British Government to grant Home Rule.

If all the Irish M.P.s had agreed upon Home Rule, then the problem might have been easily solved. In the London Parliament of 670 members, only 105 were Irish. Only 81 of these belonged to Redmond's party; four of them were independent, and the remaining twenty Irish M.P.s were firmly against Home Rule. Sir Edward Carson, a well-known Dublin lawyer, led these twenty Irish M.P.s who were known as Unionists because they wanted to preserve the Union with Great Britain. The main support for the Unionists came from the north-eastern part of Ireland. They formed a minority in the whole of Ireland and they were quite determined never to become part of an Irish state.

In January 1913, the Ulster Volunteers were formed, with

O'Connell Street was officially so named since 1882, but was still commonly referred to as Sackville Street until the 1920s. Nelson Pillar, in the right-background, was the most striking public monument in the city. Note how the trams and horse-drawn 'jarveys' queue up around the pillar, the starting point for most routes around the city.

Carson as their leader. Their aim was to resist by armed force any attempt to introduce Home Rule. This bitter division in Irish opinion was one of the biggest problems facing the United Kingdom Government in 1913. It was also a very serious situation for Chief Secretary Augustine Birrell to deal with from Dublin.

The most serious and pressing political problem in Ireland in 1913 was the conflict between the Home Rule supporters and the Unionists. But there were other fresh developments as well. Since the late 1800s a sense of national identity had begun to make itself felt. Organisations like the Gaelic League and the Gaelic Athletic Association (G.A.A.) had an increasing number of supporters around the country, and their aim was to revive interest in Gaelic culture and sport. Writers like William Butler Yeats, John Millington Synge and scholars like Douglas Hyde were rediscovering Gaelic history, literature and legends. The idea of a distinct and separate Gaelic nation was growing among a small group of people.

The ideals of the Fenians from the previous century were revived in the minds of some individuals: the goal of an independent Irish state, which had absolutely no connection with Britain. In 1905 Arthur Griffith had started the Sinn Fein movement, with the aim of setting up an Irish parliament and taking this as the first step towards breaking all contact with the United Kingdom. Griffith condemned Redmond's party for taking seats in the London parliament. His policy was that all Irish M.P.s who were elected to London should refuse to take up their seats and that instead they should set up their own parliament in Dublin.

Some people went further than Griffith. The Irish Republican Brotherhood were determined to use force to set up an independent state. Their leaders, Thomas Clarke and Sean MacDiarmuida, were secretly planning for revolution. There was then little support for these groups among the ordinary people of Ireland.

In 1908, C. J. Dolan, a Sinn Féin member opposed a Home Rule candidate at a by-election in north Leitrim, but he got less than one-third of the votes. Despite this, Sinn Féin, the Gaelic League, the G.A.A. and other groups continued to work at extending their support and changing public opinion.

THE STATUS OF WOMEN

Women's rights were a topic of heated discussion throughout

Westmoreland Street, looking towards the river. The long flowing dresses of the women in the foreground were typical of the time.

the United Kingdom around 1913. Militant women were challenging their traditional status in society, and were demanding that they should be given the same democratic rights as men. Their slogan was 'Votes for Women!' However, women were widely regarded as inferior, and as unsuited to take part in 'important' matters such as the government of the country, and 'The Suffragettes' were fiercely opposed in their fight for the right to vote, by women as well as by men.

In 1908, the Irish Women's Franchise League was founded. Its aim was to force politicians to grant the vote to Irish women. Hannah Sheehy-Skeffington was one of the leaders of the new movement. Her husband, Francis, a journalist, publicised their demands in his articles. They launched a campaign of meetings, protests, petitions and demonstrations. Francis Sheehy-Skeffington was editor of a newspaper, *The Irish Citizen,* which reported on the activities of the Women's League, and attacked the politicians in the Home Rule Party for failing to support their cause.

The activities of the women became more militant as time went by. In June 1912, eight women were arrested for throwing stones at the windows in government buildings, and were sent to Mountjoy Jail. Actions such as attacking public buildings, interrupting meetings, and purposely breaking the law in order to attract attention, were the policy of the movement. As Hannah Sheehy-Skeffington said, 'If reason does not penetrate Government Departments, flints will'.

A lot of people were turned against the women's movement by their militant activities. In Britain they failed to get what they wanted and in Ireland they were treated as a curiosity making news headlines, but not to be taken seriously.

THE POSITION OF 'LABOUR'

The end of the nineteenth and the start of the twentieth centuries saw the emergence of what was called the 'Labour Movement' throughout Britain and Europe. Workers had organised themselves into trade unions and were campaigning for better wages and working conditions. Bitter disputes broke out between workers and employers. There were frequent strikes and lock-outs, and a great wave of industrial unrest hit nearly every country in Europe.

In Britain between 1900 and 1910, the labour movement

Dublin, Sackville Street.

A leisurely scene, looking down O'Connell Street from the bridge.

Countess Markievicz, a prominent figure of the time, who was involved in the Labour Movement.

developed into a strong and powerful pressure group. The "Labour Party" was formed to represent the interests of the workers in parliament. The main principles of socialism were spreading among the workers: this doctrine claimed that workers should own and control the wealth they produced. Socialists in different countries called on all workers to unite against their bosses and rulers, and to claim power for themselves. A minority of socialists felt that an armed revolution of workers was essential. In Britain and in Europe, the rights of the working classes were slowly being established without a revolution. The trade unions were effective in improving the position of workers through the use of tough bargaining and strikes where necessary.

Ireland seemed to be an exception to this general pattern. The labour movement was slow to gain a footing although leading socialists had thought of Ireland as a country where the sparks of socialist revolution could have been fanned into fire. In Great Britain, the trade union movement grew most quickly amongst skilled industrial workers. Apart from the Belfast region, Ireland had little heavy industry at that time and so the trade unions developed slowly. The general workers, without any special training were often employed on a casual basis, and consequently they were not in a strong enough position to join together to form a trade union. Skilled workers did form their own craft unions, but they were only a small proportion of the total number of workers in the country.

By the end of the nineteenth century, there was only a small number of Irish workers organised in trade unions. At the time of the first Irish Trade Union Congress there were about ninety-three unions in the country, representing 17,476 workers — a tiny percentage of the total workforce. Only around the industrial area of Belfast did trade unions build a stronghold. In Dublin some craft unions did exist: for instance, the masons' union could trace its records back almost two-hundred-and-fifty years. Even so, their membership was small — the masons' union membership was estimated at no more than two hundred in the entire country. Most of the stronger unions were British based, as unions like the National Union of Dock Labourers had a membership extending throughout the United Kingdom. Belfast, Dublin and Cork all experienced labour troubles in the years 1907 to 1909 as workers tried to exert their power through union organisation, but most workers in the country did not belong to any union. As a result, the labour movement was a minor force in Irish life and the

Grafton Street, Lower, showing a group of Dublin policemen marching up past Trinity College.

leaders of the unions in this country recognised this fact. The Belfast Labour Party was set up in 1903 to represent workers in politics, but trade unionists in the rest of the country were not very concerned about the operation of parliament. Most labour leaders felt that it was more useful to work with the M.P.s already elected rather than putting up their own candidates.

So, when Augustine Birrell consulted with the British Government about the many problems of Irish life, he did not consider the question of labour to be a major one. The "Irish Problem" seemed to be totally different from problems within Britain itself.

DUBLIN – CITY OF THE EMPIRE

While the great events of international affairs rarely touched the lives of ordinary Dubliners, the city still enjoyed occasions of pomp and glory. Visits by the King and Queen were the greatest of these occasions, and such visits occurred in the early years of this century.

In July 1907, King Edward VII and his family paid a visit to the city, and the event was a memorable one. Landing in Kingstown Harbour, he paraded in triumph into the city and on to the Phoenix Park where he stayed with Lord and Lady Aberdeen in the Viceregal Lodge. Cheering crowds lined the streets, flags waved and bunting flew over the royal procession. It was a great occasion for the people of the city, rich and poor alike. James Plunkett, in his novel *Strumpet City,* described how a servant girl felt about the visit, and the excitement which gripped her and others:

'A band was approaching, unseen but faintly heard. Horses stamped and pennants, at a great distance, tossed in orderly file above the heads of the crowd. A cheer began, travelling through the street until those around Mary joined in. It was overpoweringly warm as the heat of packed bodies augmented the blaze of the sun. Yet there was a communicated excitement too which drew Mary to her toes... Kings built great cities and that was why there were aristocrats and gentry and after them business people and then shopkeepers and then tradesmen and then poor people like Fitz and herself. Who would give work if there were no kings and gentry and the rest? No one ever said anything about that.

The band was now directly in front, so that now and then, between shoulders and heads, she caught the sudden flash of sun

1   Their Majesties crossing O'Connell Bridge on their return from the Garden Party, July 11th, 1911.   [La fayette.

The great excitement caused by Royal visits is caught in this photograph of King George and his entourage crossing O'Connell Bridge on their return from a garden-party, July 11th, 1911. Flags and bunting decorated the streets during their visit. Cheering and waving Dubliners, like those in the right foreground, showed their appreciation wherever they went.

on the instruments. The roar of the people became louder and everybody said the King and Queen were at that moment passing. The men took off their hats, the crowd tightened and tightened. Mary looked behind and saw students clinging to the railings of Trinity College. They wore striped blazers and whirled their flat straw hats over their heads. Some of them were skylarking, of course, as young gentlemen always did on such occasions. One of them even had a policeman's helmet wherever he had managed to get it. Mary felt the pressure easing and heard the notes of the band growing fainter, but the rhythmic chorus of carriage wheels over paving setts continued. People stopped cheering and talked to each other.'

Edward's visit was memorable for another reason. The Crown Jewels of Ireland, worn by the British monarch on each visit to the country, had been stolen from Dublin Castle only a few days before the King arrived. The robbery of the jewels — worth more

17

THE KING'S LETTER

DUBLIN CASTLE,
12th July, 1911.

I cannot leave Ireland without at once giving expression to the feelings of joy and affection inspired by the wonderful reception which the people of Dublin have just given to the Queen and myself.

Wherever we have gone we and our children have been welcomed with a spontaneous and hearty loyalty that has greatly touched our hearts and made a permanent impression upon us. Without effort and without restraint, and in obedience to what seemed a natural impulse of good-will, the entire populace, men, women, and children, came out into the streets and parks to give us a true Irish welcome. We shall never forget it.

We greatly admired the decoration of your streets, and feel grateful for the efforts we know were made in all parts of the City to add to the pleasure of our visit.

Looking forward, as we do, to coming amongst our Irish people again, and at no distant date, and repeating in other parts of the country the delightful experiences of the last few days, we can now only say that our best wishes will ever be for the increased prosperity of your ancient capital, and for the contentment and happiness of our Irish people.

George R. I.

TO THE IRISH PEOPLE

On his departure fro[m] Dublin, King George, w[ho] had been deeply touched [by] his reception, left the follo[w]ing message to the people [of] Ireland.

than £50,000 — was a topic of conversation for a long time afterwards and the scandal was never explained.

Three years later, King Edward died. His son George V succeeded to the throne and the coronation took place in June 1911. He and his family embarked on a special Coronation tour of the kingdom, Dublin being one of the first cities they visited. *The Times* of London commented that it was fitting that this should be so, as the Irish people loved to demonstrate their loyalty to the Crown. George's visit was similar to his father's four years before, and the people of Dublin did indeed show their appreciation of the occasion. *The Irish Times* devoted its entire front page to a "céad míle fáilte" to the royal family. There were some people who objected to the idea of welcoming an English king on Irish soil but most were glad of the opportunity to celebrate and did not think deeply about the political issues involved. When he left Dublin, George took with him the memory of a quiet and peaceful city of the kingdom.

2
Images of Dublin

DUBLIN: POEM (By 'N', 1912)

Throughout the summer dusk the dusky city
Lies weary unto death, but knows no rest:
The folding star, like some bright eye of pity,
Holds watch above her towers to the west;
From all her wandering and foot set free,
Still constant to her first and single quest,
The strong, slow river seeks the stronger sea
And bears the ships away upon her breast.

IF YOU HAD visited Dublin in the early 1900s you would have found it a beautiful city, distinguished by the Georgian buildings of Merrion Square and Fitzwilliam Square, by the elegance of places like Pembroke Road and the glamour of Grafton Street, by gracious parks in the suburbs, and by fine houses and estates on the outskirts of the city. The population was growing, and the urban area spreading out. In 1900 an act was passed to extend the city boundaries to include Clontarf, Drumcondra, Clonliffe, Glasnevin and Kilmainham. The most striking growth occurred along the sea coast in the south east. By 1911, over 400,000 people lived in the city and suburbs.

Better transport systems made it possible for wealthy families to move out of their city centre houses and to buy or build new houses in the suburbs. The excellent train service from Kingstown to the city centre, and the tramlines that serviced a wide area, enabled people to work in the city while living in the suburbs. James Plunkett's novel, *Strumpet City* is set in Dublin about this time. In one scene, Mr. Belton Yearling, a character in the story,

19

takes a train from his home in Kingstown into the centre of Dublin, and thinks about his city:

'He liked travelling by train, especially on the Kingstown line. He liked the yachts with coloured sails in the harbour, the blue shape of Howth Hill across the waters of the bay, the bathers and the children digging sandcastles. These were pleasures to look at in the last hours of an August evening. Yearling loved his city, her soft salt-like air, the peace of her evening, the easy conversation of her people. He liked the quiet crossings at Sydney Parade and Lansdowne Road, simply because he had swung on them as a schoolboy. The gasometers at Westland Row were friends of his.'

Monkstown and Blackrock became fashionable, and wealthy people built houses in these districts. Large gardens were another attraction of the suburbs whereas in town, lack of space often ruled out an elegant garden. In addition, relatively easy access to leisure pursuits such as golfing, hunting and racing, and to the sea and the mountains, contributed much to the popularity of the southern suburbs. Nonetheless, a city centre probably makes more of an impression on a visitor than the surrounding area, and in this respect Dublin was distinctly different from the large industrial cities of the United Kingdom. In Newcastle, Glasgow or Belfast, smokey factory chimneys and bustling industrial works dominated the skyline above dour red brick houses. The city of Dublin was by comparison graceful and elegant, set off by its natural setting of river, sea and mountain.

The people and the prosperity of Dublin seemed to be linked together by the different forms of transport — transport of people, and transport of goods.

Dublin was the main commercial centre of Ireland and the docks were thriving, shipping goods in and out of the country. Along the Liffey as far as O'Connell Bridge, tall-masted sailing ships, steamers and paddle-ships docked in busy clusters.

In his story *An Encounter* James Joyce wrote about two boys spending a day by the quays, around this time. They were "mitching" for the day:

'We came then near the river. We spent a long time walking about the noisy streets flanked by high stone walls, watching the working of cranes and engines and often being shouted at for our immobility by the drivers of groaning carts. It was noon when we reached the quays and, as all the labourers seemed to be eating their lunches, we bought two big currant buns and sat down to eat them on some metal piping beside the river. We pleased our-

20

Above - The busy activity of the Dublin Port is captured in this photograph of steam and sailing ships on the lower Liffey. In the small boat in the foreground two uniformed men — possibly customs officials or pilots — make their way to the quayside.

Below - The trainline from Dublin along the south-east coast to Kingstown and Dalkey was an important factor in the spread of suburban housing. Here, the Dalkey train is shown passing Seapoint.

SEAPOINT. Co. DUBLIN. 1699. W. L.

selves with the spectacle of Dublin's commerce — the barges signalled from far away by their curls of woolly smoke, the brown fishing fleet beyond Ringsend, the big white sailing-vessel which was being discharged on the opposite quay. Mahony said it would be right skit to run away to sea on one of those big ships and even I, looking at the high masts, saw, or imagined, the geography which had been scantily dosed to me at school gradually taking substance under my eyes. School and home seemed to recede from us and their influences upon us seemed to wane.

'We crossed the Liffey in the ferryboat, paying our toll to be transported in the company of two labourers and a little Jew with a bag. We were serious to the point of solemnity, but once during the short voyage our eyes met and we laughed. When we landed we watched the discharging of the graceful three-master which we had observed from the other quay. Some bystander said that she was a Norwegian vessel. I went to the stern and tried to decipher the legend upon it but, failing to do so, I came back and examined the foreign sailors for I had some confused notion... The sailors' eyes were blue and grey and even black. The only sailor whose eyes could have been called green was a tall man who amused the crowd on the quay by calling out cheerfully every time the planks fell: — All right! All right! ......'

Guinness was the best known company in Dublin, and their drays and barges were a common sight in the city. This is an account by one woman, remembering her days as a child in Dublin:

'Guinness's drays and barges provided a distinctive touch to the Dublin scene. When walking by the Liffey we heard the chug-chug of the latter, we made a rush to the wall urging our mother along. There we gazed in admiration at the long boat with its rows of barrels and its navy clad, peak-capped crew with the word Guinness in the large red letters across their chests. Our excitement was increased when on approaching a bridge a siren blasted and the black funnel was lowered. As the barge disappeared under the shadow arch we raced to see it reappear at the other side. On the streets Guinness's drays laden with wooden casks were drawn by powerful hairy fetlocked Clydesdale horses with brass medallions hanging from their harness. In charge were fine physiqued men, uniformed in beige, long sleeved corduroy waist coats and trousers, and black bowler hats curled up at the sides.'

Moira Lysaght: *'My Dublin'*

22

Above - Horses and drays being led out from the stable-yard at Guinness's Brewery.

Left - Guinness's barges being loaded with kegs, before moving down river to load them onto big ships at the docks. These barges and their uniformed crews were a prominent feature of city life.

The city of Dublin was policed by a special force: the Dublin Metropolitan Police. This force operated only in the city centre area. Outside this territory the Royal Irish Constabulary had responsibility for the rule of law throughout the country. The Dublin Metropolitan Police impressed everybody by their size — they were exceptionally big men. None, apparently, were less than six feet two inches, and of a similarly striking build. Each carried a baton and wore a large spiked helmet.

Another common figure on the streets was the lamp lighter, who lit and put out the gas lamps with a crook-ended stick. Electric street lighting was introduced in Dublin in 1892, but most streets still retained the gas lamps.

'The most sensational spectacle by far was the passing of the Fire Brigade. Its approach was heralded by the loud clanging of its bell, and the traffic stood still to give clear passage to the galloping horses, drawing the great red chariot, as it seemed to me. The sight of its long ladders, coils of hose-pipes, shining brasses and above all its brass-helmeted fire men standing erect on either side; all filled the onlookers with awe and admiration. Following it in a horse-drawn, self driven gig came the chief, Captain Purcell, a well known figure. A less dramatic spectacle, but one which drew a large crowd, was the annual Life Boat procession. A big feature was full sized boats mounted on horse-drawn floats which paraded through the streets.'

Moira Lysaght: *'My Dublin'*

Most of all, perhaps, the trams of Dublin remained in the minds of all those who visited the city. The trams were a very important aspect of life in Dublin. Without a doubt these "galleons of the street" made an impressive sight.

'On a wet, stormy night when the theatre crowds were making for home, they were a truly stirring sight converging at Nelson Pillar. Up to a hundred trams would be on the move in Sackville Street, bells clanging, crossing and recrossing tracks, each in its halo of yellow light with sparks flashing from the trolley head, distinctive blue, green, yellow or red identification lights and illuminated multi-coloured signs claiming special attention. When heavily loaded the trams dipped and swayed like trawlers on a choppy sea and the emergency fenders under the conductor's and motormen's platforms (to push anyone who fell on the tracks clear of the wheels) made a mighty clatter as they scraped and crashed on the stone setts at every dip of the tram.'

J. Quaney: *'A Penny to Nelson's Pillar'*

ONE OF THE "GIANT" POLICE,
O'CONNELL STREET, DUBLIN

Top - A picture of one of the "giant" members of the Dublin Metropolitan Police, taken in O'Connell Street.

Above - Golf was growing to be an immensely popular game in the early days of the century. Of particular interest are the various dress-styles; notice, for instance, the bare-footed grubby-faced caddy on the right.

The Dublin United Tramways Company had been founded in 1896, operating horse-drawn trams. From January 1900 electric trams were used and the last horse-drawn trams were taken off the road on January 13th, 1901. (This last journey on the Sandymount line was an eventful one, because a 'gentleman's gentleman' was knocked down at the corner of Shelbourne Road, and broke both his legs – the driver and conductor were arrested). From 1913 on, symbols were used on trams to indicate the various routes – for instance the Dalkey Tram had a large green shamrock, the Terenure Tram a red triangle. At night the trams were lit by a special coded lighting system to identify each different route. There was a big pool of workers in the Tramway Company, a large proportion of them being part-time. It was a policy of the company to keep these part-timers as a "spur" to the full-time staff who knew they could easily be replaced if their work was unsatisfactory.

'The tram men who were invariably of country stock, were always fully uniformed even to the peaked cap. Many of the conductors were noted for their running comments as they called out stopping points, adding their own explanatory definitions such as 'St. ....'s Road, Lodger's Alley'; 'St. Kevin's Hospital – a rose by any other name would smell as sweet'; while they punched the oblong cardboard tickets which varied in colour according to the amount of fare.'

Moira Lysaght: *'My Dublin*

The tram-fares did not rise between 1896 and 1914. One of the busiest routes was the Dalkey Line: the fares from Sackville Street along this route were as follows –

Sackville Street to Haddington Road		...	:	1d.
Merrion Gates	...	...	...	:	2d.
Blackrock	...	...	...	:	3d.
Kingstown	...	...	...	:	4d.
Dalkey	...	...	...	:	5d.
Return fare Dalkey/Sackville Street		...	:	8d.

Dublin was the first city in the world to have a roofed upper-deck tram service, but most trams remained uncovered. Smoking was permitted on the open deck upstairs, but not "inside" as the lower saloon was called. The only exception to this was the Howth trams, which had a special partition "inside", to allow smokers their pleasure on the extra-long journey. The tramlines were

26

described by one man as being like 'arteries to Dublin's life', and Dubliners came to depend greatly on the service, particularly those who lived in the suburbs but worked in the city.

The Terenure Tram passes through Rathmines on a sunny afternoon.

3
The Affluent City

You have often been styled 'Happy-go-easy'. Don't be ashamed of the title. Glory in it. It's rare. And surely in this twentieth century it's a mighty good thing and a mighty fine thing to be happy at all.

William Dawson, 1912: *'My Dublin Year'*

AMONG THE WEALTHY, life at this time was becoming more exciting than ever. The arrival of the motor car for instance, brought an entirely new aspect to the world of transport. Instead of depending on trains and trams, well-off citizens could now use their own private transport for travelling long distances quickly. Cars were of course expensive but they were growing in popularity.

'Rapid motion through space elates one; so does notoriety; so does the possession of money', wrote James Joyce, and for those who were able to indulge in all three, the world could be a carnival of pleasure. Motor-racing began to rival horse-racing among the young and rich. The spread of the motor car brought with it some other effects. In the newspapers of the time, reports like this began to appear more often:

KNOCKED DOWN BY A MOTOR
The Magistrates at Cabinteely Petty Sessions yesterday investigated a charge preferred by District Inspector Murphy against Patrick J. Long of Anglesea Road, Dublin, of having recklessly driven a motor car on the 14th September and knocked down and seriously injured a labourer named Christopher McCabe, on the road to Cabinteely.

Mr. Long was fined 20/- and charged with costs for the appearance. A summons for grievous bodily harm was withdrawn.

Freeman's Journal Thursday December 12th, 1912

Advertisement hoarding on Church Street, showing a cross-section of products. Of particular interest are the advertisements for the theatres, circus and horse-racing, the most popular forms of entertainment at the time.

For the more adventurous, travel to foreign lands had become more common than before. Young people, particularly, took frequent trips to London and other cities in Britain, and some continental countries. Yachting cruises around the British Isles were also a feature of life among the rich. The latest fashion styles were noted and quickly copied in the best circles in Dublin. It was very important to be dressed stylishly. A person's social position was much more readily detected from his or her appearance than it is today. Well dressed men wore quiet-coloured clothes — dark suits, stiff shirts and ties. It was an essential part of being well-dressed to have a hat and gloves at all times when out of doors. For women, even more than men, the style of dressing was an essential part of personality. The well-dressed lady would appear in a long, fairly narrow skirt and her elegant appearance would be crowned by a large, eye-catching hat.

Social life among the 'best' families in Dublin had a very definite pattern, and as already mentioned revolved around the social activities of the Viceroy and his wife, Lord and Lady Aberdeen. It was a great honour to be on the Viceregal list for party invitations. There was a regular 'season' of party-going, and plenty of society magazines to comment on who was there, and the relative merits of each gathering. In addition to the private parties and dances organised by individuals, going to the races and to the theatre were important social events of the year.

The early years of the century was a good time for Irish theatre. Dublin was lucky to have seven theatres operating regularly in the city — the Gaiety, the Theatre Royal, the Tivoli, the Empire, the Queen's, the Rotunda and the Abbey. New actors and writers were emerging who were deeply involved with Irish drama, and it was at this time that figures such as W. B. Yeats and J. M. Synge were becoming well-known at home and abroad. Their efforts were to make Irish theatre world famous, but in the meantime the most popular theatrical entertainment was much less serious, and the best received performances were of musical comedy and variety shows. Travelling acts were added to the regular "bill-of-fare" at the variety theatres, and the large audiences clapped — and sometimes hissed — with great vigour.

Cinema was beginning to make an impact on the entertainment scene. Films were shown regularly in cinemas such as the Rotunda Picture House, near the Parnell Monument, the O'Connell Street Picture House and the Phoenix Picture Palace. They were often in a serial form, and one episode was shown each

day or each week, known as the "follier-upper". The film (a silent movie) was normally accompanied by a pianist, and sometimes by a small orchestra playing in the picture house. James Joyce, later to become a world-famous writer, was one of the earliest film enthusiasts, and was for a short time manager of the first commercial cinema in the city, the Volta in Mary Street.

WEALTH AND WORK IN DUBLIN

Dublin had a few large industries, and so very few people gained wealth through actually manufacturing goods. Instead, the city was a commercial centre: that is, a city of trade, buying and selling goods. It was in this way that most rich Dublin business-men made their money and it was also in this respect that the city was different from the industrial cities of the United Kingdom.

The docks were of special importance. Goods arrived at Dublin docks from all over the world and were sent on, usually by rail, to destinations throughout Ireland. Raw materials, such as timber, and clothing materials like linen, were common imports, while grain, poultry and even tobacco were among the exports from the port. The main industries in the city were based on foodstuffs. Guinness's Brewery was the biggest and best known of these, and was closely identified with the 'character' of the city. Jacobs' Biscuit factory was another well-known family business.

As well as being the focal point in the country's commercial life and communications, Dublin was the centre of administration. The Chief Secretary and his staff at Dublin Castle controlled a large network of administrators who lived in the city and its suburbs. These civil servants made up an important segment of the Dublin middle classes. The middle classes were comfortable, satisfied and conservative. They had fairly well-paid jobs, secure employment and good housing. The civil servants, bank officials and various other 'white-collar' workers saw themselves as being the backbone of Dublin's life.

There were people who were less well-off, but who were also reasonably content. For instance, those who were employed at Guinness's Brewery were thought to have very enviable jobs. This firm had a reputation for treating its employees extremely well. Similarly, jobs with the Dublin United Tramways Company and with some large stores were seen as highly desirable, even though the wages were sometimes lower than their counterparts in other British cities.

32

Top - Idrone Terrace, Blackrock. This shows the choice of transport available to residents in this fashionable suburban area. The trainline was of great benefit to those working in the city, while the jarveys afforded a more leisurely form of travel. Trams and, increasingly popular, private cars were also used.

Above - A tram makes its way down a quiet North Circular Road towards the Phoenix Park. The houses shown were typical of the upper-middle-classes of the time.

HOUSING IN DUBLIN

The bulk of the new suburban houses built since the mid-nineteenth century were homes for the wealthy. These houses were usually not quite as big as the old Georgian homes of the rich in the city centre. Houses were graded in the census of the time, from "first-class" to "fourth-class" according to their size and the materials used in their construction. Red brick was a feature of new buildings of the time, and houses were generally made with high quality natural materials: slated roofs, granite sills and wooden sash windows. Iron railings and the occasional use of stained glass and tiles were also in fashion.

It was quite common for the very wealthy families to have domestic staff who 'lived in' with the family. To have a male domestic servant was a sign of very high social standing. He would usually have been a gardener or a chauffeur. Even less affluent middle-class families often had a maid or a cook who lived in the house. Newspapers of the time carried many advertisements for household servants — most of the positions were taken by girls from the country, although Dublin men and women were also employed.

ANOTHER SIDE OF LIFE

While life was pleasant enough for the well-to-do, they themselves were only beginning to be aware that not everyone in the city was so fortunate. Great interest was taken in matters of public importance such as the issues of Home Rule, women's right to vote, business and trade, and now the question of poverty also became a topic for serious comment and discussion. It was becoming clear to more and more people that, amidst all the comfort in Dublin, there existed absolute poverty on a wide scale. The conditions under which the poor were living were not generally known among the privileged people of Dublin, but there was an uneasy awareness that great problems existed in the city. Various government enquiries had shown up poverty on a massive scale, especially in the centre of the city. Some drainage and re-housing schemes had been introduced but they had no great effect on the situation. Life, for the poor of the city, was an endless cycle of "cast-off scavenging" dependent on the unwanted possessions of the rich.

'In the mornings, just at the breakfast hour, the poor searched

The poor of Dublin got most of their clothes at
second-hand markets, like this one in Horseman Row.
The cast-off clothes of the rich, like the hats and
coats shown in the foreground, were all they could
afford — and even then, such purchases were rare.

diligently in the ashbins of the well-to-do for half-burnt cinders and carried sacks and cans so that as much as possible of the fuel might be salvaged. The ashbin children were pinched and wiry and usually barefooted. They lived on the cast-offs. They came each morning from the crowded rooms in the cast-off houses of the rich; elegant Georgian buildings which had grown old and had been discarded. The clothes they wore had been cast-off by their parents, who had bought them as cast-offs in the second-hand shops in Little Mary Street or Winetavern Street. If the well-to-do had stopped casting-off for even a little while the children would have gone homeless and fireless and naked.'

James Plunkett: *'Strumpet City'*

That description of winter for the poor in Dublin would not have been recognised as real by large numbers of the well-off. Yet the truth was beginning to spread.

Newspapers published letters from readers on various topics and in this way discussion and argument could be carried on, on any subject of current interest. In 1913, there was an argument in the columns of *The Irish Times* over wages and conditions of workers in English factories. Much abuse was thrown at English 'sweaters' — employers who paid their workers low wages in very bad conditions. On May 13th of that year, a letter appeared from someone who signed himself, or herself, 'Ignorant': 'I have been told that in Dublin certain classes of workers are miserably under-paid. If this is so, can we in our glass-houses throw stones at English "sweaters"? ' It was a genuine question from one who was genuinely ignorant. The lack of knowledge of "certain classes of workers" was typical of most of the wealthy class in Dublin at that time. The question remained unanswered in the newspaper, but a reply came on the streets of the city before the year was out.

Two young boys pose for the camera, dressed in clothes many sizes too big for them. Their poverty can be seen by the strange array of female hand-me-down clothes.

37

4
The Tenement City

Ireland is a country of wonderful charity and singularly little justice. And Dublin, being an epitome of Ireland, it is not strange to find that Dublin, a city famous for its charitable institutions and its charitable citizens, should also be infamous for the perfectly hellish conditions under which its people are housed, and under which its men, women and children labour for a living.
— *James Connolly*

IN THE YEAR 1913, a series of events occurred which made clear for all to see the dreadful conditions of poverty in Dublin. No one could avoid the unpleasant truth any more. On the evening of Tuesday September 2nd 1913, at about a quarter to nine, two houses in Church Street collapsed without warning, burying the occupants. They were four storey buildings, with shops on the ground floor. The sixteen rooms upstairs were occupied by about ten families, over forty people. Seven people were killed in this disaster and many more were injured. Many of the victims had been standing or sitting in the doorway and street when the front wall of the houses suddenly collapsed, burying them in the rubble. Rescue parties worked through the night digging people out. Mrs. Maguire, who occupied a room in one of the houses that collapsed, described the scene:

'I was standing in the halldoor of the house, looking at the children playing in the streets. Other women were sitting on the kerb-stone so as to be in the air. Suddenly I heard a terrible crash and shrieking. I ran, not knowing why, but hearing as I did a frightful noise of falling bricks. When I looked back I saw that two houses had tumbled down. I did not know what I did then but I remembered rushing. There was a heap of bricks and stuff piled

38

Left - A street scene in Dublin, showing two young girls possibly on an errand to get milk or simply water in the jug carried by one of them. In the background, a bowler-hatted gentleman appears to be reprimanding a boy: certainly, the onlookers are interested in the incident.

Below - Drying clothes was always a problem in the tenements, and this photograph of a dirty alley (Henrietta Buildings) shows how some slum-dwellers coped with the problem.

up on the street, where a moment or two before children were playing and women sitting, watching them.'

This disaster showed people far more than words would ever do, the dreadful conditions under which thousands were living. Most people were shocked that such an event could occur but some of them were not surprised. Mr. R. G. Pilkington of the Dublin Citizens Association Committee on Housing wrote in *The Irish Times* that 'the mass of the citizens are in ignorance of the real wants of the city... We have evidence to show that (owing to dilapidation) what recently happened in Church Street may occur in other parts of the city.'

A Committee of Inquiry which was set up by the government to study housing in Dublin, showed that what Mr. Pilkington had written was true. This Committee reported its findings in 1914 and presented a picture of appalling poverty in the tenement areas. These tenement houses, found mainly around the centre-city area, used to be the houses of the rich before the rich began to move to the suburbs, or indeed to England. The Committee defined 'tenement houses' as : 'Houses intended and originally used for occupation by one family but which, owing to change of circumstances, have been let out room by room and are now occupied by separate families, one in each room for the most part.'

There were just over 400,000 people living in Dublin and of these, 87,305 lived in tenement houses in the centre of the city. Even more alarming was the fact that eighty per cent of the families living in tenements occupied only one room each.

An anonymous poet of the time writing in a magazine, *The Irish Review* was struck by the great contrast between the sheer squalor of life in the city slums and the beautiful countryside only a few miles from the city centre. For all the nearness, they might have been two different worlds.

> *And children, faring to far fields forlorn*
> *Forget her squalor for a single day*
> *To break great branches of the blossoming thorn;*
> *Or strip, and in the cooling water play.*
> *Or gather cowslips; till at dusk, footworn,*
> *Returning home, each court and narrow way*
> *Is fresh with flowers from the meadows borne —*
> *But in the stifling slums they soon decay.*
> *— 'Dublin', by 'N'*

Visits to the "far fields" of the countryside were very rare for children of the slums, however.

Tenement buildings in bad repair at Angle Court. The pump in the foreground was the only source of water. Washing and drying clothes was a continuous problem. There are twenty-three women and children shown in the photograph: when the menfolk and older children not shown are considered, one gets an idea of the conditions under which people struggled in the city.

Life in the tenements was limited and confined. According to official classification, 22,701 people lived in "third class" houses which were termed as unfit for human habitation. In contrast to this, one inspector described a first-class tenement house at 41 Camden Street Lower occupied by five families, consisting of twenty persons, as follows: 'It has one water closet, is in good repair and I regard this as a first-class tenement'.

Jim Phelan, who lived in a tenement, describes how his father overcame one of the daily problems of life —

'We lived in a single room, in a huge tumble-down slum tenement. Next door a similar vast slum house had long since fallen down... Living in a tenement, and having no land or garden, nor even a yard, naturally the drying of clothes and so on was difficult. To my father... that problem was easy of solution. He built two strong spars from the two windows of our place, to carry clothes-lines. Projecting them twelve feet, each carried a cross-piece at the end, with a pulley at either extremity, by which a clothes-line could be manoeuvred in and out.

'Sixty or seventy feet above ground-level, and on top of a hill, this made a marvellous drying-ground for clothes. My mother was the envy of the slum.'

Reporting on the conditions in the tenements, the Committee said —

'There are many tenement houses with seven or eight rooms that house a family in each room and contain a population of between forty and fifty souls. We have visited one house that we found to be occupied by 98 persons, another by 74 and a third by 73. The entrance to all tenement houses is by a common door off either a street, lane or alley, and in most cases the door is never shut day or night. The passages and stairs are common and the rooms all open directly either off the passages or landings. Most of these houses have yards at the back, some of which are a fair size, while others are very small, and some few houses have no yards at all. Generally the only water supply of the house is furnished by a single water tap which is in the yard. The yard is common and the closet accommodation is to be found there, except in some few cases in which there is no yard, when it is to be found in the basement where there is little light or ventilation.

'The closet accommodation is common as the evidence shows, not only to the occupants of the house, but to anyone who likes to come in off the street, and is of course common to both sexes. The roofs of the tenement houses are as rule bad....

A girl sleeps beneath a bundle of clothes while her sister stands by the door of their tenement flat. Note the toilet bowl in the corner: sanitary facilities were dreadful in the tenements, usually consisting of no more than one W.C. in the yard, to be shared by all the tenants in the house.

No. of Case.	Situation of room.	Number of rooms held by family.	Number of family (resident members only, including lodgers).	Occupation of head of family.
32	Top front	1	3 (no lodgers) ...	Charwoman ...
33	Top back	1	4 ...	Labourer (out of work owing to strike).
34	Two-pair front	1	4 (widow, son, 2 daughters).	Casual work when able to get it.
35	Two-pair back	1	3 ...	Works in Barrington's soap factory.
36	Front drawingroom.	1	6 (one lodger) ...	Charwoman ...
37	Back drawingroom.	1	3 ...	Labourer (locked out).
38	Front and back parlours.	2	6 (no lodgers) ..	Electrician ...
39	Front kitchen	1	6 ...	Labourer ...

10 rooms in house (back kitchen vacant). In every case accommodation inadequate for number in house, sole water tap being in yard, only one
Rooms investigated, 9.
Families resident, 8.

An example of the conditions in one tenement in Dublin taken from a paper read by D. A. Chart to the Statistical & Social Inquiry Society of Ireland in 1914.

Occupation of any other working (resident) members of family.	Total weekly earnings of family.	Rent per week.	Remarks (presence of sickness, state of room, &c.).
		s. d.	
—	6s. to 7s. ...	2 0	Occupier out, hence information scanty. Walls and ceiling in good order.
—	16s. to 19s. when working.	1 9	Papers and ceiling in good order. Information scanty, as the mother was out.
Son, bookbinding apprentice. One girl in Jacob's, 7s. to 11s. a week (now 2s. 6d. strike pay). Other girl, laundry, 4s.	11s. to 15s.	3 0	Walls and ceiling in good order.
"The girl, 1s. 6d."	Man, 22s. to 28s. per week	2 0	Walls and ceiling in good order. Room very clean, but poorly furnished. Man drinks.
—	8s. to 11s. ...	3 0	Walls and ceiling in good order. Room clean and well furnished.
—	16s. to 19s.	2 0	Walls and ceiling in good order. Room clean, but very poorly furnished. Everything pawned. Decent man.
—	30s. to 40s.	5 0	Walls and ceiling in good order. Well and completely furnished.
Mother "charing"	—	2 6	Not admitted; further information refused by daughter acting on mother's orders.

not in proportion to rent, while water and sanitary arrangement quite lavatory. Yard very well kept, stairs rather dirty.
Inhabitants recorded, **35**.
Total weekly rental, 21s. 3d.

45

Church Street Dublin 1913. These propped-up buildings are similar to those referred to on the two previous pages.

'Having visited a large number of these houses in all parts of the city, we have no hesitation in saying that it is no uncommon thing to find halls and landings, yards and closets of the houses in a filthy condition, and in nearly every case human excreta is to be found scattered about the yards and in the floors of the closets and in some cases even in the passages of the house itself.'

A witness before the Committee described a dwelling he had seen: 'One room measuring about ten feet square, with a small closet off it: contains absolutely no furniture. The family of nine (seven children) sleep on the floor, on which there is not enough straw for a cat, and no covering of any kind whatever.' The interiors of the tenement rooms were very sparsely furnished. The basic items were bedsteads, bed-clothes, tables and chairs (though boxes were often used instead for the last two items). 'In some tenement rooms the bedstead is not to be seen in its usual place in the corner, but in its stead there is spread on the floor a mysterious and repellent assortment of rags, which few inquirers have had the hardihood to investigate and which is believed to serve as a bed,' wrote D. A. Chart.

Frequently, whatever possessions a family owned would be pawned in times of special hardship. Many families regularly pawned belongings at the beginning of the week to be redeemed at the end of the week when more money came into the home. 'The number of articles pawned in Dublin is very large,' wrote one observer. 'From inquiries which I made some years ago, I ascertained that, in a single year, 2,866,084 tickets were issued in the city of Dublin.'

HUMAN CONDITIONS

The effect of such housing conditions on people was very great, both physically and mentally. A man who visited various tenements in the city relates two of his outstanding memories:

'One is of a "front-drawingroom" on a sultry day in August. A child lay ill with whooping cough and was lying exhausted on the bed after a paroxysm of coughing. Flies were numerous in the room (it was a hot summer) and were passing and repassing from the food on the table to the face and body of the sick child.

'Another is of an indignant father who appealed to me, as one in temporary authority, to procure the ejection of a suspected "unfortunate" from the room above his own. He said he was trying to "bring up his children dacint" and how could he do it

47

This painting, by Stan Cowen, shows the interior of Kavanagh's Pub, Hogan Place, Dublin. Through the front door, a man can be seen unloading a keg of beer from a dray, while in the background, across the street is shown a 'fan-light' door, typical of many around the city. Many pubs of the time had a grocery section attached to the bar, though this feature is not shown in this picture.

Top - At Summerhill, near Gardiner Street, a group of mostly barefoot children stand with a woman. Deaths of children under the age of one year made up 20% of deaths in the city, in a normal year. In 1913, they accounted for more than 25% of all deaths; Sir Charles Cameron, the chief Medical Officer for the city, blamed the lack of sufficient food and warmth caused by the great lock-out for this alarming increase.

Above - This tenement room in Newmarket Street cost 2s.0d. a week in rent. The bare floorboards and scant furniture were typical of the Dublin tenements. A half-eaten loaf of bread lies on the table while cooking utensils are scattered on the floor. Clothes hang to dry near the fireplace, while an oil-lamp is hooked onto the wall.

with women like that in the house.'

The terrible living conditions resulted in many serious social problems. Alcohol played a very large role in the lives of many. Workers who drank too much were left with little money to spend on the needs of their families. This problem was made worse by the custom, in some areas, of paying workers their wages in pubs. It was not only men who were inclined to seek satisfaction in alcohol. Many grocery shops were situated within pubs, and this meant that the temptation for women to drink was always present. Alcohol offered an easy escape from the everyday troubles of life in the tenements.

Crime was widespread, and was often connected with drunkenness. In Dublin, the figures for serious crimes — like murder, rape and larceny — were 100 crimes for every 10,000 people. (This was much higher than most cities in the United Kingdom).

Another great social problem was the high rate of prostitution. Many women were forced into this through poverty: it was the only way they could get badly needed money. At night, O'Connell Street and Grafton Street were well-known areas for prostitutes to gather. Indeed, a custom grew in O'Connell Street whereby one side of the street was reserved for "respectable" people and the other side for prostitutes. The position of women generally was worse than that of men. A girl of a tenement family was forced to grow up very quickly: at a time when a girl in the suburbs was taking part in the pleasures and sports of teenagers, the working-class girl was often forced to act as a mother to her younger sisters and brothers.

The overcrowded tenements did not allow people the simple dignities of life. Any form of personal privacy, for instance, was nearly impossible. Despite this, people still spoke of the great "spirit" which existed among people in the slums. Friendliness and charity were very strong features of the community. Such a spirit was hard to keep in the bad times, however, and it was never a real substitute for decent housing, a reasonable wage and a healthy diet.

FOOD IN THE SLUMS

'The daily fare of the labouring classes is characterised by extreme monotony and this circumstance alone goes far to account for the drinking habits of some of our people.' (D.A. Chart, 1914).

50

The average wage for tenement dwellers in 1913 was about 18/- a week: this meant that a man, wife and family would be forced to rely on a very meagre diet to survive from week to week. A typical breakdown of a weekly budget for a tenement dweller would have looked like this:

	s.	d.
Rent		
Rent	2	6
Fuel and Light	2	0
Bread	4	0
Tea	0	9
Sugar	0	8
Milk (usually condensed)	0	6
Butter (Dripping, Marg.)	1	6
Potatoes (or other veg.)	1	0
Meat, Fish, Bacon, etc.	2	0
Total	14	11
Wages for Week	18	0
Balance	3	1

The normal diet was barely enough to maintain life — it did not provide much nourishment. Meat was a rarity and was only purchased if money was left over. Fruit or puddings were never seen. Meals were as follows: BREAKFAST — Tea and Bread (sometimes with butter, dripping or margarine); TEA (or Supper) — The same as above; DINNER — Potatoes, cabbage, onions. Sometimes bacon or herrings.

In many cases, even this budget would be too generous. Often men would be out of work, or fuel prices might be higher, or extra expense would arise: in such cases there was no option but to 'do without'. The 3/1d. left at the end of the typical budget for a family with four children, had to provide clothes, furniture, general amusements and other odd items.

Some sample cases from *The Irish Worker,* 4th November, 1911:

'A FAMILY, man and wife, resides in Dame Court. His occupation is that of a tailor but he can earn only 10s. a week. His rent is 2s. 6d. which leaves 7s. 6d. for food, fuel, light, clothes, bedding, etc. Their breakfast consists of dry bread and tea. They have only another meal, dinner and supper combined; it consists of dry bread and tea and herrings, and occasionally porridge.'

51

'LABOURER — Aged 40; has wife and three children; usual earnings 15s. a week; when working full time earns 18s.; average weekly expenditure on fuel 9s. 6d.; rent of room 2s.; fuel and lighting 1s. 3d. Daily dietary consists of tea, bread, butter, dripping, potatoes — bacon for husband, and sometimes a little fresh meat; on Sundays, pig's cheek and cabbage. Husband suffers from a delicate chest in the winter and is consequently sometimes without employment.'

Barefoot children passing the time on the cobbled street.

'FIELD LABOURER — Six in family; earns 14s. 6d. a week. Rent of room 2s. 6d.; weekly expenditure on food 9s.; fuel and lighting 1s. Friendly Society subscription 8d. weekly — a teetotaller. Daily diet consists of tea, bread, butter, dripping, potatoes. On Sundays, the principal meal consists of bacon and cabbage.'

HEALTH

Bad housing conditions, bad sanitation and poor diet gave rise to major health problems in tenement districts. There were several 'killer-diseases' widespread throughout the city. The most common and most dreaded of these was T.B. or 'consumption' as it was commonly known. The poor living conditions were seen as directly responsible for about one third of the deaths registered in Dublin between 1902 and 1911.

FROM PUBLIC HEALTH REPORT – DUBLIN, 1913

Cause of Death	No. of Deaths
Fever	73
Typhus	13
Measles	29
Whooping Cough	86
Diphtheria	90
Croup	4
Influenza	93
Dysentery	4
Tuberculosis (T.B.)	1,444
Cancer	521
Nervous, Circulatory, Respiratory, Digestive Diseases (e.g. Pneumonia, Diarrhoeal Diseases etc.)	4,642
Other Diseases	1,436
Violence	204
DEATHS FROM ALL CAUSES	**8,639**

DEATHS: 1902-1911

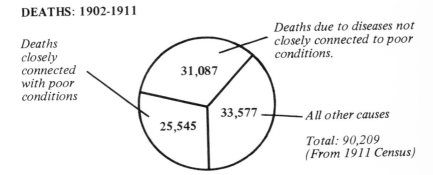

Deaths closely connected with poor conditions

Deaths due to diseases not closely connected to poor conditions.

31,087

25,545

33,577 — All other causes

Total: 90,209
(From 1911 Census)

Some of these diseases — measles and whooping cough, for example — were highly contagious, spreading rapidly from one person to another. Overcrowding in the slums meant that these diseases were all the more dangerous and difficult to avoid. The bad food and toilet facilities led to widespread diarrhoeal diseases and T.B. Damp and cold conditions in the tenement houses also contributed to the number of people suffering from pneumonia. Other diseases and sicknesses — for instance, nervous illnesses connected with blood circulation — were not directly caused by the poor living conditions. However, tenement dwellers living in damp, overcrowded houses and with a poor diet were often not strong enough to withstand these illnesses.

Certainly, being poor increased the chances of an early death. Public Health Reports were regularly issued and the figures they gave showed the great gap between the health of the rich and the health of the poor. This was seen most clearly when the deaths registered in the city were studied according to social class. The professional and middle classes (doctors, lawyers, civil servants, etc.) had the lowest early death rate, while the 'General Service Class' (ordinary workers) and the casual workers like hawkers and labourers had the highest early death rate.

OCCUPATION OR SOCIAL POSITION	NO. OF DEATHS FOR EVERY THOUSAND PEOPLE
Professional Class	18.1
Middle Class	15.1
Lower-Middle Class	16.8
General Service Class	21.3

The most alarming aspect of the health problem was the high rate of infant mortality — large numbers of babies died. Sir Charles Cameron, the Medical Inspector for Dublin, said 'It is certain that infants perish from want of sufficient food', and the figures he produced to support this argument were shocking:

Total No. of deaths registered, 1911	9,118
Deaths of infants under 1 year	1,808

About twenty per cent of all deaths in the city occurred among those less than a year old: nearly all of these occurred among the poorest classes. Even for those infants who did survive their first

Men at work at the junction of Gardiner Street and Dorset Street, laying a drainage pipe. Headgear was commonly worn, even at work. Notice also, on the building on the left, the statue holding three balls — the symbol of a pawnshop, an important place in the lives of thousands of Dubliners.

year, life was bound to be difficult. Reared in absolute poverty, they were all the time threatened by the killer-diseases common in the city and were usually without the nourishment necessary to combat these.

EMPLOYMENT

The lack of manufacturing industry in Dublin meant that there was an unusually high number of unskilled workers employed in various jobs, mainly those to do with the distribution and transport of goods. By the nature of things these jobs were very often of a 'casual' nature: steady employment was never taken for granted. Some employers felt that tenement-dwellers made bad workers because they were physically weak — indeed people from the country would often be picked for casual labour before a tenement dweller. An English journalist, Arnold Wright, looked at people living in the tenement slums from the point of view of an employer, and wrote: 'It cannot be overlooked, that the very nature of their mode of living tends to reduce their value to the labour market... they speedily lose, not merely their sense of self-respect, but their capacity for sustained exertion.'

There were about 90,000 adult males in Dublin, according to the census of 1911. With a naturally growing population swelled by others from the country coming to live in the city, the number of available workers was always greater than the number of jobs to be filled. The result was a high rate of unemployment, sometimes as much as twenty per cent. Only 10,000 were apprenticed to some trade in the city. Aside from these, the large number of unskilled workers competed with each other for the scarce jobs, with the result that wages remained very low.

UNSKILLED LABOUR IN DUBLIN – 1911

General Labourers	17,223
Carters, Draymen, etc.	3,081
Messengers, Porters, etc.	4,604
Total unskilled	24,908

Note: The word 'unskilled' describes workers like labourers, carters and dockers, who were so described around this time. It does not mean that they had no skill at their work: merely that they did not belong to any recognised trade or craft.

A Guinness worker shown at one of the "taps" in the brewery. One of the attractions a job in Guinness offered was the practice of giving each worker a free pint of stout each day. As can be seen from the sill in front of him, this worker was not the first to avail of this offer!

Occupations of Heads of Families Occupying Tenement Houses in the City.

Occupation	No.	Occupation	No.	Occupation	No.
Actor	1	Cattle Dealer	2	Factory Worker	377
Agent	44	Cattle Drover	91	Farm Steward	1
Antique Dealer	1	Caretaker	154	Farrier	28
Army Servant	1	Cap Maker	3	Farrier's Helper	1
Artisan	4	Cellar Man	1	Fat Sorter	1
Artist	5	Chain-maker	1	Feather Cleaner	1
Asphalter	1	Chandler	3	Feather Sorter	1
Attendant	31	Charwoman	1,195	Ferryman	1
Accountant	1	Chauffeur	38	Field Worker	32
Auctioneer	1	Checker	24	Firewood Maker	10
		Chef	6	Fireman	48
		Chemist	2	Firesman	1
Bacon Curer	3	Chicken Butcher	5	Fisherman	3
Bag Maker	10	Chimney Cleaner	14	Fishmonger	3
Bake House Worker	2	China Repairer	2	Fish Curer	2
Baker	158	Cigarette Maker	2	Fishing-net Maker	1
Bailiff	1	Cigar Maker	1	File Maker	1
Barber	86	Cinema Operator	1	Fitter	147
Barber's Assistant	11	Civil Bill Officer	1	Foreman	14
Basket Maker	24	Civil Servant	1	Forewoman	2
Bellows Maker	3	Cleaner	1	Fore Staller	3
Bell Ringer	1	Clerk	223	Framemaker	7
Bicycle Mechanic	1	Clerk of Works	1	Fruit Dealer	2
Billiard Manager	1	Clock Maker	2		
Billiard Marker	13	Cloth Cleaner	1		
Bill Poster	9	Clothier	2		
Bird-cage Maker	1	Clothes Presser	1	Ganger	1
Blacksmith	119	Coach Builder	33	Gardener	51
Blacksmith's Helper	11	Coach Maker	5	Gas Inspector	2
Blind Maker	9	Coach Trimmer	3	Gas Worker	1
Boarding House Keeper	4	Coachman	44	Gilder	6
Boatman	4	Coal Factor	11	Glass Worker	1
Bobbin Winder	1	Coal Porter	100	Glazier	15
Body Maker	19	Coal Heaver	3	Glass Finisher	1
Bog Oak Carver	16	Cockleman	1	Goldbeater	1
Bog Oak Turner	1	Cockle Seller	2	Groom	31
Boiler Maker	34	Coffin Maker	6	Gun Repairer	1
Boiler Maker's Helper	1	Collar Maker	2	Gun Smith	1
Boilerman	13	Collector	4	Gut Cleaner	2
Bookbinder	51	Colourman	5		
Bookfolder	27	Commission Agent	22		
Book-keeper	8	Commercial Traveller	3		
Book-maker	12	Compositor	86	Hair Dresser	23
Book Seller	3	Common Lodging House Keeper	11	Ham Agent	1
Boot Closer	6			Hatter	4
Boot Maker	364	Contractor	9	Horse Dealer	3
Bottle Blower	19	Confectioner	26	Harness Maker	47
Bottler	2	Conductor	13	Horse Shoer	1
Bottle Washer	2	Cook	63	Horse Clipper	3
Bottle Worker	1	Cooper	80	Hose Maker	1
Boxer	1	Corn Porter	3	Hosiery Worker	1
Box Maker	18	Cork Cutter	6	House Agent	2
Brassfinisher	17	Cork Sorter	1	House Keeper	29
Brassmoulder	1	Corset Maker	2		
Brasspolisher	1	Crane Man	8		
Brassworker	5	Cutler	8		
Bricklayer	195	Cycle Engineer	1	Ice Cream Maker	4
Brush Maker	19	Cycle Fitter	1	Ice Cream Vendor	1
Bung Maker	1	Copper Smith	3	Insurance Agent	13
Butcher	123			Inspector	1
Butler	8			Instructor	1
Barmaid	1			Iron Moulder	7
Builder	1	Dairy Boy	63	Iron Worker	15
Burnisher	1	Dairy Proprietor	19		
		Dealer	646		
		Driller	1	Jeweller	3
		Dispatch Clerk	1	Jewel Case Maker	1
Cabinet Maker	67	Domestic Servant	134	Jewellery	1
Cabinet Fitter	1	Dock Policeman	1	Jewellery Worker	1
Candle Maker	2	Draper	3	Joiner	2
Canvasser	5	Draughtsman	1	Journalist	1
Captain	4	Dressmaker	357		
Cardboard Box Maker	11	Drover	3		
Car Driver	92	Dyer	10		
Car Owner	31			Labourer	9,542
Car Man	151			Laundry Worker	112
Carpenter	359			Lamp Lighter	14
Carpet Cleaner	2	Egg Sorter	1	Laundress	11
Carpet Layer	6	Electrician	41	Lace Maker	3
Carpet Planner	8	Electric Plater	1	Lady's Maid	1
Carpet Worker	3	Engine Driver	59	Lath Maker	1
Carriage Cleaner	2	Engine Cleaner	2	Leather Agent	1
Carrier	8	Engine Washer	1	Leather Dresser	4
Carter	339	Engineer	11	Legging Maker	1
Case Maker	14	Engraver	3	Lead Worker	2

previous page - The table is taken from the Report of the Departmental Committee on Housing Conditions of the Working Class in the City of Dublin, 1914.

Dwarfed by towering tenements and crumbling houses, a group of slum-dwellers stand on a derelict site at North Cumberland Street.

For women, the position was even worse. While the average labourer's wage worked out at less than one pound a week, the average female worker earned about half that. For instance, in Jacobs, one of the city's biggest employers, women earned from 7s. to 15s., depending on their position. The most usual job for women was that of domestic servant in the homes of the wealthy. Because there were few other jobs available for women, families rarely had the extra income that working women could have provided.

WOMEN WORKERS 1911

Domestic Servants	13,551
Dressmakers and Milliners	4,294
Seamstresses & Shirtmakers	1,296
Tailoresses	1,000
Charwomen	1,246
TOTAL	21,387

5
Workers and Employers

It is sometimes said that the movement calls out the man, whilst in many cases there is much to be said for the proposition that the man makes the movement.   *The Leader,* September 1913.

THE MAJOR INDUSTRIAL CITIES of the U.K. had developed a familiar appearance: skylines jagged with countless factory chimneys, a constant pall of smoke overlying the city, closely packed terraces of workers' houses. Such features were rare in Dublin. For many, visitors as well as citizens, the absence of heavy industry added to the city's attractions. For others, however, it made life more difficult. The large number of unskilled workers, with no choice but to accept casual low-paid work, were in a very weak position to demand better pay and conditions. Employers could tell applicants for a job to "take-or-leave" the terms they offered, knowing that there were plenty of others to take the job instead. In such a situation, workers too often saw their colleagues as a threat to their own security. They lacked the power and confidence of organised, skilled workers, such as were common in Britain and Europe. Trade unions were thus very weak in Dublin.

It was into this situation that James Larkin, an official of the National Union of Dock Labourers, came in 1907. For the next seven years he was one of the main forces in the life of the city and, in the process, made many friends and enemies. The writer, Sean O'Casey, wrote of him: 'God grew sorry for the work-worn people and sent another man into their midst whose name was Larkin.' On the other hand, Larkin himself told the story of how a priest once said of him: 'The anti-Christ has come to town.' One way or the other, he certainly made a deep impression on the

*'The chief who raised the red-hand up
Until it paled the sun;
And shed such glory o'er our cause
As never chief has done.'*

Liberty Hall became the headquarters of the I.T.G.W.U., and was the scene of much frenzied activity in years up to and after 1913. Large crowds regularly gathered in front of the building to hear Larkin deliver his fiery speeches from an upstairs window. This photograph shows Liberty Hall in 1916, destroyed by shellfire in the course of the rising of that year.

The great regard of the Dublin workers for Larkin was captured by the verse above, written on a banner beneath a portrait of their leader, and carried proudly in procession through the city. The "Red Hand" was the symbol of the Irish Transport & General Workers Union.

people.

James Larkin was born in Liverpool in 1876, the son of parents who had emigrated from Armagh in search of employment. He started work after his father's death, when he was only eleven years old. He worked at a number of different jobs before becoming involved with the National Union of Dock Labourers (N.U.D.L.) while working on the docks in Liverpool. He quickly attracted attention as being a great organiser, enlisting hundreds of dock-workers in the union. As a result, he was made a full-time official of the union. His job as organiser for the union sent him to Scotland first, then to Belfast and then on to Dublin, Cork and Derry before he finally settled in Dublin. A powerful and inspiring public speaker, he made an enormous impression wherever he went. In all the cities where he worked, he helped organise workers, usually involving himself in bitter strikes.

He became deeply involved in labour troubles in Dublin and Cork, so much so that he began to embarrass the leaders of his own union. While attempting to organise the general workers in Dublin, he finally pushed his own superiors too far. In December 1908 he was sacked from his £4-a-week job as organiser for the N.U.D.L. Larkin was not too worried. He was now committed to the cause of building up a strong union among the Dublin general workers. To this end he gathered around him some other members of the N.U.D.L. and other unions and formed a new Irish-based union. Sean O'Casey described the occasion, which occurred on January 4th, 1909: 'In a room in a tenement in Townsend Street, with a candle in a bottle for a torch, and a billycan of tea, with a few buns for a banquet, the Church militant here on earth, called the Irish Transport and General Workers Union, was founded'.

Due in the main to Larkin's own personal appeal, membership of the union grew to around 10,000. His tremendous ability as an orator and his obvious compassion for the oppressed made him the hero of thousands. Among his close colleagues, he was admired but not always liked personally. People like James Connolly — a leading socialist who returned to Ireland from the United States and became an official of the new union — Thomas McPartlin, W. P. Partridge and others all worked hard with him in building up the union, but they often resented his arrogant and often angry manner. Larkin was never an easy man to get on with. However, these problems were set aside in their total commitment to the new union.

Liberty Hall became the headquarters of the I.T.G.W.U.,

Head of Jim Larkin by Mina Carney, the wife of one of his best friends.

and the centre of all the union's activity. Larkin also wanted a newspaper to speak for the workers of the city and, in 1911, *The Irish Worker* was published and appeared every week under his editorship. Larkin himself at this time lived with his wife and three sons in Auburn Street in Dublin, paying nine shillings a week rent. His weekly wage as General Secretary of the Irish Transport and General Workers Union was £2 10s., which he gave to his wife to spend as she thought fit. (He never touched alcohol but was fond of smoking cigars and occasionally a pipe).

RECRUITMENT VERSE —
The Irish Worker 20th July, 1912

J   oin us at once
I   heard him say
M any a man was lost thro' delay

L inger not, as the time it flies
A nd your chances are slipping away
R un to your friends at Liberty Hall
K eep the wolf from your door, I say
I   n a year or so hence you'll not regret —
N o, you'll only be proud of his name I'll bet.

W.S.C.

Many of the older Trade Unions, especially in Belfast and Cork, had bitter rows with the new organisation, which was breaking so many of the old accepted rules. Even some of Larkin's sympathisers regretted some of his more extreme acts and sayings — his quick temper, his rash decisions, his cruel insults.

The new union was involved in notable strikes in Cork and a six-months dispute in Wexford in 1911. It was fast becoming the most feared enemy of Irish employers, and, in particular, of the leading businessman of the day, William Martin Murphy.

LARKIN'S CAMPAIGN AGAINST ALCOHOL

Larkin, a teetotaller,was firmly opposed to alcohol, and his newspaper *The Irish Worker* frequently warned readers of the dangers involved in frequenting the public house.

In 1913, reflecting on the appalling conditions that existed in Dublin, Larkin said: 'When I came to Dublin, I found that the men on the quays had been paid most of their wages in public houses, and if they did not waste most of their money there, they would

A view of O'Connell Bridge from Bachelors' Walk. The Carlisle Building in the background was the site of "The Irish Independent" offices, owned by William Martin Murphy, since 1905.

not get work the next time. Every stevedore was getting 10 per cent of the money taken by the publican from the worker, and the man who would not spend his money across the counter was not wanted.'

Through his anti-alcohol campaign, Larkin became greatly loved by wives and mothers in the city, who felt the brunt of their menfolk's squandering on drink, or "bung" as it was called.

WILLIAM MARTIN MURPHY

William Martin Murphy was born in Bantry, Co. Cork in 1845. His father owned a building contracting business, but died when William was only nineteen years old. At that early age he took over the family business and guided it successfully through years of immense growth. He had a natural talent for the world of commerce and he acquired great wealth through business deals extending from London to Africa. By the early 1900s, William Martin Murphy had become the foremost Irish businessman. Unlike his counter-parts in Britain, Murphy had little involvement with industry as such. His own personal business empire was built on trade and commerce rather than manufacture; in this he was typical of most Irish businessmen. Murphy's wealth and fame lay in his ownership of or interest in such enterprises as Clery's Department Store, the Imperial Hotel, the *Irish Independent* newspaper and the Dublin United Tramways Company.

Because of his powerful position in the business world, Murphy had immense authority.. In 1911 Murphy was the main force behind the formation of the "Dublin Employers Federation Ltd.". This was a group of employers who came together to discuss common action in the face of unions like the I.T.G.W.U. (A Cork Employers Federation had already been successful against Larkin's activities in 1909.) He was greatly respected by his fellow-employers in the Dublin Chamber of Commerce. He had a reputation for being a good employer, who gave his workers fair wages. However, he could not tolerate his workers disputing with him. Although he claimed to be in favour of trade unionism, he refused to recognise the I.T.G.W.U., and would not employ anyone who was a member of that union. Naturally there grew a great personal hatred between himself and Larkin, the leader of the rebel union.

In his private life, Murphy was a man of quiet tastes. He took great pleasure in sailing his yacht off the coast of Cork. He took little part in the social life of Dublin and was not highly regarded

Irish Life, 10th October, 1913.

Social Announcements.

The marriage arranged between Captain E.
Blakiston-Houston, 8th Hussars, fourth son
of John Blakiston-Houston, Esq., Orangefield,
Belfast, Co. Down, and Dorothy Irene, eldest
daughter of Lieutenant-Colonel F. W. Rea,
29th Infantry, will take place at Sehore, Cen-
tral India, on October 18th.

A marriage has been arranged, and will
shortly take place, between Mr. John Knox
Thompson, M.B., Matmore, Lisburn Road,
Belfast, second son of the late Mr. John
Thompson and Mrs. Thompson, Ellerslie,
Windsor Park, Belfast, and Miss Marguerite
Hassard, Innismore, Delgany, younger
daughter of the late Mr. and Mrs. John Hassard, San Angelo, Texas, U.S.A., and grand-
daughter of the late Mr. John Connor, Delgany, Co. Wicklow, and Eccles Street, Dublin.

The marriage is announced to take place on
New Year's Day, in Singapore, between Capt.
Wm. Agnew Moore, Royal Garrison Artillery,
and Violet, youngest daughter of the late
Robert Lyon Moore, D.L., of Molenan, Derry,
and Mrs. Moore, Cliff, Belleek, Co. Fer-
managh.

The marriage arranged between Arthur
Purefoy Irwin Samuels, M.A., Barrister-at-
Law, only son of Arthur Warren Samuels,
K.C., 80 Merrion Square, Dublin, and
Dorothy Gage Young, only daughter of
George Lawrence Young, J.P., Culdaff House,
Co. Donegal, and Millmount, Randalstown,
Co. Antrim, will take place shortly before
Christmas.

William Martin Murphy on his way to attend
a strike inquiry court at Dublin Castle, from
'Irish Life' a society magazine of the period.

Left - An extract from 'Irish Life' magazine
1913.

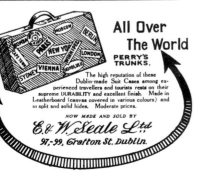

by the upper class of the capital city: there was too much of the "common merchant" about him. Murphy was well-known for his personal charity. A woman wrote in 1913 – 'Mr. Murphy is a just and kind employer. Outsiders know little of his real goodness – I experienced it myself when my husband died after a long and expensive illness. The first letter I received was from Mr. Murphy enclosing a cheque for £30 – "as my needs might be pressing" – and just asking me to say a prayer for the soul of his son who died a year before my husband, although he had never laid eyes on me or my children.'

A strong supporter of the Home Rule movement, Murphy was not by nature a "public" person. He did hold some very strong views, and never hesitated to criticise those with whom he disagreed. This was particularly true of his fellow-employers, many of whom he condemned for their ill-treatment of workers in their employment. Indeed, he blamed some employers for giving aid to Larkin's cause by not treating their workers more fairly. Murphy was a strong, aloof type of man. Wealthy, charitable, just and able, he was a loyal friend and a ruthless enemy.

James Larkin

'I am engaged in holy work. Of course, I cannot now get employers to see things from my point of view, but they should try to realise my work. I have worked hard from an early age... I have made the best of my opportunities.'

— J. Larkin, September 1913

'His was a handsome, tense face, the forehead swept by deep, black hair, the upper lip of the generous, mobile mouth hardened into fierceness by a thick moustache, the voice deep, dark and husky, carrying to the extreme corners of the earth.'

— Sean O'Casey: *Drums under the Window*

'The consequences of Larkinism are workless fathers, mourning mothers, hungry children and broken homes. Not the capitalist but the policy of Larkin has raised the price of food until the poorest in Dublin are in a state of semi-famine — the curses of women are being poured on this man's head.'

—Arthur Griffith

'Sitting there, listening to Larkin, I realised that I was in the presence of something that I had never come across before, some great primeval force, rather than a man. A tornado, a storm-driven wave, the rush into life of spring and the blasting breath of autumn, all seemed to emanate from the power that spoke.'

—Countess Markievicz

William Martin Murphy

'I am not the leader of the employers, although I have been called the leader. I seem to have gained a good deal of notoriety, but I have had greatness thrust upon me.'

— William Martin Murphy, September 1913

'If you met him, you got the impression of an ascetic kindly man of the diplomatic class, exceedingly well dressed, quiet spoken with a humorous twinkle in his eye and no trace of a Dublin accent.'

— *Daily Express*

'William Martin Murphy, a creature who never hesitated to use the most foul and unscrupulous methods against any man, woman or child who, in the opinion of William Martin Murphy stood in William Martin Murphy's way, a soulless, money grabbing tyrant.'

— *Irish Worker*

'William Murphy is a humane man, known for his personal honour and charity; a "good employer" as it is called, a successful captain of enterprise, an insensitive imagination, in short, a very dangerous opponent.'

—Tom Kettle

'The most foul and vicious blackguard that ever polluted any country.'

— James Larkin

THE WIDENING GULF

Throughout the United Kingdom, the rift between the labour movement and the employers had widened greatly in the early years of the century. Strikes had occurred frequently in many places, but entering the second decade, it seemed that industrial relations were becoming more settled. For the most part, Dublin had escaped the troubles of labour unrest. In 1900 the Dublin Chamber of Commerce had announced: 'We are pleased to note the growing disposition of all classes to unite in promoting the best interests of our country.'

As the I.T.G.W.U. grew in Dublin, it appeared that the different classes had different ideas as to what exactly those "best interests" were. As labour relations settled somewhat in the rest of the United Kingdom, strikes and lock-outs became more frequent in Ireland, and in Dublin in particular. The I.T.G.W.U. were almost always involved.

THE SYMPATHETIC STRIKE

One of the greatest sources of disagreement between employers and trade unions, was the use of what was known as the "sympathetic strike". This was a tactic often used by Larkin. A sub-committee to investigate the troubles between the employers and workers in Dublin, defined the sympathetic strike as: 'a refusal on the part of men who may have no complaint against their conditions of employment to continue work because in the ordinary course of their work they came into contact with firms whose employees have been locked out or are on strike'.

The committee, headed by Lord George Askwith, disapproved of the idea in their report: 'No community could exist if resort to the "sympathetic strike" became the general policy of Trade Unionism, as owing to the interdependence of different branches of industry, disputes affecting even a single individual would spread out indefinitely.'

A famous example of a sympathetic strike occurred in July and August 1913 when W. M. Murphy refused to employ I.T.G.W.U. members on the staff of his *Irish Independent* newspaper and sacked 100 members from the Tramway Company. Workers involved in distributing the newspaper — though not employed by Murphy — refused to handle it in protest. Messrs. Eason and Co., the large city newsagents, were asked by Larkin not to sell the paper. Eason refused to oblige Larkin. The result was that dock-workers at Kingstown refused to handle any goods from England addressed to Eason — regardless of what they may be. Mr. T. M. Healy, who represented Murphy and the employers before Askwith's committee, described the situation in this witty manner:

'Mr. James Larkin will not allow any English author to have a sale in Ireland through Easons: he would even boycott Shakespeare (laughter). Are the English trade unions that print these books to be destroyed and injured? What was the crime that Mr. Eason had committed?

'In the course of his business, Mr. Eason distributed through the country a well-known half-penny journal produced in Dublin called the *Irish Independent*. The owner of the *Independent* was the chairman of the Tramway Company. Mr. Larkin had a fight with the Tramway Company, therefore the *Independent* had to be put down, therefore Eason had to be injured and therefore Shakespeare had to be boycotted.' (laughter)

Larkin and the I.T.G.W.U., however, saw the sympathetic strike as the finest example of workers' solidarity with each other. In their eyes the bosses were always united — 'the employers know no sectionalism', Larkin said, 'the employers gave us the title of "the working class". Let us be proud of the name.' That pride could best be shown by the principle of "one-out, all-out". The sympathetic strike had the great strength of immediately showing the employers the power of the working class, and making it clear that no section could be bullied without taking-on the whole class of workers.

'The sympathetic strike,' James Connolly wrote, 'is the recognition by the working class of their essential unity.' Professor Thomas Kettle, a young M.P., a neutral observer of the battle between the employers and workers, was fairly sympathetic to the workers. However, he disapproved strongly of the sympathetic strikes referring to them, with contempt, as "strikes-by-telephone". However, another neutral observer, Rev. Walter McDonald, a Professor at Maynooth College, condemned the hypocrisy of employers who complained about the sympathetic strike. Referring to the agreement of 404 employers not to employ I.T.G.W.U. members, Prof. Rev. McDonald wrote: 'See how the employers have acted in Dublin: they have no qualms of conscience in having recourse to the sympathetic lock-out'.

6
The Divine Mission of Discontent

I care for no man or men. I have got a divine mission, I believe, to make men and women discontented.   *James Larkin*

DUBLIN WAS UNIQUE in that the interests of employers and workers were so vividly represented by their leaders, Murphy and Larkin. Murphy refused to recognise the I.T.G.W.U., and refused to talk with anyone who was a member of that union. In the light of this opposition, the union set about enlisting many of the workers in Murphy's companies — especially in the Tramways Company and in the *Irish Independent*. These tactics had to lead to a confrontation with Murphy and the other directors.

Amid rumours of strike and sackings, Murphy called a meeting of his employees in the Tramways Company on Saturday July 19th, 1913. The purpose of the meeting was to dissuade the workers from joining the I.T.G.W.U. He did this through a mixture of flattery and threats:

'I want you to clearly understand that the directors of this Company have not the slightest objection to the men forming a legitimate Union. And I would think there is talent enough amongst the men in the service to form a Union of their own, without allying themselves to a disreputable organisation, and placing themselves under the feet of an unscrupulous man who claims the right to give you the word of command and issue his

---

Note:
In some accounts, the term "strike" has been used to describe the industrial dispute in Dublin in 1913. In this account the word "lock-out" is used, since the employers' refusal to employ I.T.G.W.U. members was the basis of the trouble. The word "strikers" is used to describe the general body of workers locked-out, in this context.

orders to you and to use you as tools to make him the labour dictator of Dublin... I am here to tell you that this word of command will never be given, and if it is, that it will be the Waterloo of Mr. Larkin.

'A strike in the tramway would, no doubt, produce turmoil and disorder created by the roughs and looters, but what chance would the men without funds have in a contest with the Company who could and would, spend £100,000 or more. You must recollect when dealing with a company of this kind that every one of the shareholders, to the number of five, six or seven thousands, will have three meals a day whether the men succeed or not. I don't know if the men who go out can count on this.'

Later the directors of the company issued a statement to the public, in answer to the many rumours and suggestions common in the city: 'The Directors are well aware of the attempts being made by James Larkin to foment disturbance among the men, which, however, have met with little success. The company have no apprehension of any trouble with their employees and are prepared to meet any emergency that may arise.'

Despite this, though, the directors were becoming worried at the increasing influence of Larkin's men among their staff. As the I.T.G.W.U. continued to attract new members, it became clear that stronger action was required. Accordingly, on the 21st of August, 1913, about 100 workers in the Tramways Company received the following notice: 'As the Directors understand that you are a member of the Irish Transport and General Workers Union whose methods are disorganising the trade and business of the city, they do not further require your service.'

This was a direct challenge to the I.T.G.W.U. Meetings of workers were called by Larkin but it was obvious that there could only be one reply to Murphy's challenge. From the point of view of the union, Murphy and his fellow directors had started a lockout: the workers could only respond with a total withdrawal of labour. Larkin carefully chose the moment to strike. He delayed the call to cease work until the time of greatest impact. So it was, that shortly before 10.00 a.m. on Tuesday, August 26th, 1913, trams around the city stopped in their tracks: drivers and conductors got out. Dublin was plunged into a bitter labour dispute. The date was well chosen, for on that day The Dublin Horse Show began, and the city was crowded with visitors. Thus the action would create the maximum amount of disruption.

'On a bright and sunny day, while all Dublin was harnessing

LEAF FROM A DUBLIN DIARY, AUGUST 1913

TUESDAY 26 AUGUST — *R.D.S. Horse Show opens*

10.AM Larkin calls out ITGWU members. Trams stop in their tracks on the streets of Dublin

WEDNESDAY 27 AUGUST — *Ladies' Day at Horse Show*

Scuffles + fights on the streets between strikers police and 'scabs'

THURSDAY 28 AUGUST — *Parties connected with Horse-Show in full swing.*

Larkin and four others arrested for libel and conspiracy. Tension is high in the city

FRIDAY 29 AUGUST — *Horse-Show reckoned to be the best ever.*

Police ban meeting to be held on Sunday in O'Connell St. Larkin released on bail, burns the order paper at a meeting at Liberty Hall

SATURDAY 30 AUGUST — *Horse-Show over for another year.*

Riots in the city. Police baton charge crowd at Eden Quay. Two men are killed. James Nolan and another whos name is not yet known

SUNDAY 31 AUGUST

O'Connell Street is packed with people wondering will Larkin appear at the banned meeting. He does. Violence in the streets as police charge the crowds. Larkin is arrested.

itself into its best for the Horse Show, the trams suddenly stopped. Drivers and conductors left them standing wherever they happened to be at a given time in the day when the strike commenced.... They came out bravely, marching steadily towards hunger, harm and hostility, just to give an answer for the hope that was burning in them.'

— Sean O'Casey: *Drums under the Windows*

In his play *Big Jim,* James Plunkett pictures a typical incident of that day:

SCENE: A TRAM STOP ON THE DALKEY LINE.
Two well-off gentleman halt a passing tram.

1st Gentleman: Conductor — does this car go to Ballsbridge?

Conductor: Well, sir, it does and it doesn't, sir.

1st Gentleman: What the devil do you mean?

Conductor: Well now, sir, it's hard to explain. But you might as well take the weight off your legs anyway. Hold the rail. *(The bell rings. The conductor continues).* Fares please. *(He punches a ticket).*

2nd Gentleman: Better call the fellow again.

1st Gentleman *(calling):* Conductor... Does this car go to Ballsbridge or does it not?

Conductor: That more or less depends on the time, sir.

1st Gentleman: What the deuce can the time have to do with it? You either go to Ballsbridge or you don't.

Conductor: Tell me the time and I'll tell you the answer.

1st Gentleman: The time is exactly.... ten o'clock.

Conductor: Then it doesn't, sir.

2nd Gentleman *(to 1st gentleman):* You see — incorrigible!
(to Conductor): May I ask what you are putting in your button-hole?

Conductor: My Trade Union Badge, sir. The Red Hand. I'm not allowed wear it on duty.

1st Gentleman: Then what the devil are you putting it in your buttonhole for?

Conductor: Because I'm no longer on duty, sir. I'm on strike. *(Shouting)* Hey, Puddiner! It's ten o'clock!

Driver: Wha.......?

Conductor: It's ten o'clock.

Driver: Right — me beauty. We stop where we are! I'll take off the trolley.

1st Gentleman *(unbelievingly)*: On strike...? In Horse Show Week — !''

In fact, only a small number of workers walked out: about 700 of the 1700 in the company. On the evening of the first day of the strike, Jim Larkin spoke to the striking tramway workers outside Liberty Hall.

'This is not a strike, it is a lock-out of the men who have been tyrannically treated by a most unscrupulous scoundrel... If one of our class should fall then two of the others must fall for that one. We will demonstrate in O'Connell Street. It is our street as well as William Martin Murphy's. We are fighting for bread and butter. We will hold our meetings in the street and if any one of our men fall, there must be justice. By the living God, if they want war, they can have it.'

The city was filled with tension for the following days. Strikers resented the workers who continued to operate the trams, and fights often took place between them.

'... many of the men on strike were noticeable in the streets during the day. They still wore their uniform though they are under obligation to return them to the company. They also sported badges depicting a red hand the symbol of the Irish Transport Workers Union.'

The Irish Times, Thursday, August 28th, 1913.

'... an attack was made on one of the tramcars at Arran Quay. The glass panelling of the car was smashed by missiles thrown by a group of toughs on the sidewalk. Two bricks and a bottle were thrown at the car, and they crashed through the windows, some of the passengers having narrow escapes.'

The Irish Times, Thursday, August 28th, 1913.

OODSHED IN DUBLIN.

APPALLING SCENES IN CITY

FIERCE BATON CHARGES.

HUNDREDS INJURED.

TWO MEN DEAD.

HOSPITALS OVERCROWDED.

LARKIN ARRESTED

O'Connell Street, 'Bloody Sunday' 31st August 1913.

Many clashes with the police occurred, and fierce baton charges resulted in numerous injuries. This reached its peak on Saturday night when, after a particularly brutal police charge, in the city centre one man, James Nolan, lay fatally injured. Stephen Gilligan who was at the scene of the charge, described what he saw:

'I was going down to the post office with a telegram. As soon as I landed outside I saw the charge of the police. The people were talking in threes and fours, and got no chance of moving. The first thing they knew was the batons coming down on them. I heard a voice saying, "Now give it to them, boys!" I pretended I was a reporter and got safe. I saw the police charge the doorway and smash the sidelights. They charged round Eden Quay. The majority went on the footpath charging the people there. The people for the most part kept to the quayside. I stood in the shadow of the Corporation weigh-house and saw poor Nolan trying to get away. I saw a police constable, 224C, Constable Bell, strike him with a baton. I saw him fall on his knees. The constable ran on, and then 149C struck him across the neck. I went back towards the Butt Bridge.'

So great was the outcry arising after these events that a special committee was set up to investigate the behaviour of the police. This committee summed up its findings, as follows: 'We desire to report in conclusion that in our opinion the officers and men of the Dublin Metropolitan Police and the Royal Irish Constabulary, as a whole, discharged their duties throughout this trying period with conspicuous courage and patience. They were exposed to many dangers and treated with great brutality.... The total number of constables injured during these riots exceeded 200.'

On August 28th, Larkin and four of his comrades had been arrested on charges of libel and conspiracy. They were released on bail. It had been announced that Larkin would address a meeting in O'Connell Street on Sunday the 31st August, but the authorities issued an order banning the assembly. On Friday night Larkin publicly burned a copy of the order and encouraged his listeners to fight any attempt to stop the meeting.

Sunday at midday saw people begin to gather on O'Connell Street, in expectation of something, though no one was quite sure what. Larkin, disguised with a beard, entered the Imperial Hotel — owned by Murphy! — opposite the G.P.O. He appeared at a balcony window on the first floor, and caught the attention of the crowd. As he had promised, he spoke to them briefly, before leaving the window. Uproar broke out on the street below. Larkin was promptly arrested. The police, in panic attacked the crowd in heavy baton charges.

'Oh! O'Connell Street was a sight of people on that Sunday morning! From under the clock swinging pedantically outside of *The Irish Times* offices, across the bridge over the river, to well away behind the Pillar, topped by Nelson, the wide street was black with them; all waiting for Jim to appear somewhere when the first tick of the clock tolled the hour of twelve.'

Sean O'Casey: Drums under the Windows

'I was in O'Connell Street one evening when Jim Larkin, to keep a promise, appeared on the balcony of the hotel, wearing a beard as a disguise. He spoke amidst cheers, and hoots for the employers. Police swept down from many quarters, hemmed in the crowd, and used their heavy batons on anyone who came in their way. I saw women knocked down and kicked — I scurried up a side street; at the other end the police struck people as they lay injured on the ground, struck them again and again. I could hear the crunch as the heavy sticks struck unprotected skulls. I was in favour of the strikers.'

Ernie O'Malley: On Another Man's Wounds

Jim Larkin in disguise following his arrest at the Imperial Hotel.

SIX TRAMS ATTACKED

Violent scenes were associated in an attempt made by a crowd, about 5.30 p.m. to force the motormen of six trams to give up their driving handles in Camden Street. The conductors were also asked to leave their cars. Both the drivers and conductors refused to comply with the demand of the crowd, who then flung stones and missiles at the cars, and at the drivers and conductors.

There were only a few policemen on the scene at the time, and they were vigorously stoned by the crowd. Reinforcements soon arrived, together with six mounted policemen, who were summoned from O'Connell Street, and at least six baton charges were delivered on the crowd before they were finally dispersed.

A large number of people were seriously injured in the course of the baton charges, including a number of respectable spectators, who were in no way identified with the riots.

TRAMCARS ATTACKED ON QUAYS

In the afternoon a unique and sensational incident occurred on the Quays, in the vicinity of Church Street, when a man was seen to jump into the Liffey. It was low water at the time. Two policemen, who were stationed at the bridge, hastened to his assistance. As soon as they had left their place of duty, a crowd, which had quickly collected, availed of the temporary absence of the police to attack a passing tram, and smashed its windows. It is believed that the incident was a ruse to divert the attention of the policemen from protection duty.

OTHER RIOTS

Rioting also broke out in Gardiner Street and Sheriff Street, North Wall, Henry Street, Mary Street, South Wall, and in the whole district from Christchurch to Inchicore. Several baton charges and large numbers injured. A number of plate glass windows were broken in the city.

WATERFORD STREET SCENE
An Old Woman Battered

Some violent scenes were witnessed in Waterford Street about 6 o'clock. It appears some persons flung stones and bricks at police. The police charged the crowd, who sought protection in a house, and followed them inside. It is reported that the male members of the family and the mother, an old woman, were attacked in the excitement. A number of arrests were made.

Freeman's Journal, Monday, 1st September 1913.

For the next week, Dublin was in a state of great unrest. Meetings of workers were held around the city, especially at Liberty Hall, the nerve-centre of the workers movement. The funeral of James Nolan, the worker killed beneath the police batons, took place on Wednesday 3rd September. It was an impressive event, as striking workers walked in silence through the city streets behind the horse-drawn hearse. That night, another meeting was held in Liberty Hall. Since his arrest at the Imperial Hotel on Sunday, Larkin had been held in Mountjoy Jail. In his absence an important figure of the British labour movement, Keir Hardie, spoke. Hardie urged the Dublin workers to stand together against the employers, and he believed that the British Trade Unions would support them in their stand.

On the same night as Hardie spoke so strongly to the union members, William Martin Murphy, on behalf of 404 employers, announced the decisions reached by a special meeting of employers:

AGREEMENT

We hereby pledge ourselves in future not to employ any persons who continue to be members of the Irish Transport and General Workers Union and any person refusing to carry out our lawful and reasonable instructions or the instructions of those placed above them will be instantly dismissed no matter to what union they belong.

The Viceroy's party for the Horse Show, posing on the steps of the Viceregal Lodge. Phoenix Park.

The lock-out was absolute now. Dublin workers — in various jobs and regardless which union, if any, they belonged to — received the following document to sign:

"I hereby undertake to carry out all instructions given me by or on behalf of my employers, and further, I agree to immediately resign my membership of the Irish Transport and General Workers Union (if a member) and I further undertake that I will not join or in any way support this union."

Angered by this document, thousands of workers refused to sign. Many who were not even members of the I.T.G.W.U., could not sign it in conscience, even though they had no dealings with Larkin or his Union. James Connolly wrote of one such case:

'A labourer was asked to sign the agreement forswearing the Irish Transport and General Workers' Union, and he told his employer, a small capitalist builder, that he refused to sign. The employer, knowing the man's circumstances, reminded him that he had a wife and six children who would be starving within a week. The reply of this humble labourer rose to the heights of sublimity. "It is true, sir," he said, "they will starve; but I would rather see them go out one by one in their coffins than I should disgrace them by signing that." And with head erect he walked out to share hunger and privation with his loved ones. Hunger and privation — and honour. Defeat, bah! How can such a people be defeated? His case is typical of thousands more.'

Dublin was set for a struggle, which was to last for longer than most people thought.

"OLYMPIA, IN ALL ITS GLORY..."

Yet, in some circles in Dublin, life continued as usual. The lock-out served as no more than an interesting topic of conversation for some people. On the day that Larkin called his I.T.G.W.U. members out on strike, the Dublin Horse Show was opening at the Royal Dublin Society grounds in Ballsbridge. This was the greatest occasion in the year for Dublin "society". The events happening on the streets had little effect on the Show and the parties surrounding the event continued as in every other year.

The Irish Times captured some of the feeling of the Show, in its report on Thursday, August 28th: 'Olympia in all its glory could not excel the spectacle presented yesterday afternoon in the

84

Some House Parties for the Horse Show.

At the Viceregal Lodge the Lord Lieutenant and the Countess of Aberdeen are entertaining a large number of guests, amongst whom are the American Ambassador, Mrs. and Miss Page, the Yuvarajah of Mysore and his suite, the Earl of Carrick, the Countess of Kimberley and Miss Capell, Lady Dorothy Howard, Lady Leucha Warner, Lord and Lady Charnwood, Sir Anthony and Lady Weldon, Sir Nugent and Lady Everard, Mr. and Mrs. Brittain, Mr. W. Hozier, Mr. Vincent Baddeley, Dr. and Mrs. Gauvein.

⊙   ⊙   ⊙

Sir Arthur and Lady ᵀ
Royal Hospi⁺⁻'
minster, the
of Fingall aɪ
of Kenmare, .
Marshal Sir
and Captain ɪ

At Killakee
Somerset and L
Castlemaine, Cᴄ
Mr. and Hon. '
Vansittart, Mr.
Clements, Miss ,
Captain Robertsoɪ
Mr. Spencer Guinn

⊙

Lord and Lady P
Powerscourt this wᴇ
Countess of Rosse,
Vesci, Mr. and Mɪ
Muller, Mrs. Leslie, ɑ

⊙   ⊙

At Knockmaroon F
and Lady Evelyn Gu
Lord Dalmeny, Sir M
General Brentwood, Mɪ
Lady Maud Hoare, Caɪ
Mr. and Mrs. Naper, a
Lloyd.

⊙   ⊙

Lord and Lady Talbot dᴄ
Malahide Castle this week
Lady Wynford, Lord and
Hon. Mary French, Sir
Lady Mahon, and Mr. Sam

⊙   ⊙

Mr. and Lady Mary Cᴄ
Rathbeale Hall includes Theɪ
Cottenham, Miss Angela Dɪ ⸻nd, Count
Paul Metternich, and Mr. Alfred Boyd.

⊙   ⊙   ⊙

At Kenmare Park, Rush, Lady Palmer is entertaining Mrs. and Miss Poole, Col. Dunn, Mr. and Miss Cotton, and Mr. Fenwick Palmer.

⊙   ⊙   ⊙

Sir John and Lady Kennedy's house party at Johnstown Kennedy includes Miss Kennedy, Mr. and Mrs. Lloyd Cruddas, Miss Coxwell-Rogers, Mr. Kennedy, and Mr. James Kennedy.

At Kilteragh, Foxrock, Sir Horace Plunkett is entertaining the Earl of Coventry, Mr. and Mrs. T. B. Ponsonby, Miss Violet Martin, Miss Cornelia Bryce, and Mr. Holroyd Smyth.

⊙   ⊙   ⊙

Sir Timothy and Lady O'Brien's house party at Grangewilliam includes the Misses O'Brien, Mr. and Miss Kingscote, Mr. A. R. Bourne, and Mr. J. G. O'Brien

⊙   ⊙   ⊙

Sir Kildare and Lady Borrowes are entertaining at Barretstown Castle this week Col. and Mrs. H. Fortescue, Mr. and Mrs. Lionel Trower, Miss R. Matheson and Miss C. Mathes⸻ Miss Heather Powles.

⊙   ⊙   ⊙

House Col. Gore Lindsay is
Morgan Lindsay and Miss
Captain Walter and Lady
Miss Macpherson, and Miss

⊙   ⊙

unboyne, Captain and Mrs.
aining Sir Hugh and Lady
oun, and Mr. Cowper.

⊙   ⊙

inteely, Judge and Mrs.
v includes Mrs. Milne
ɪd Mrs. W. D. Kenny,
in Reginald Stracey,
ɪrd, Captain Archibald

picturesque grounds of the Royal Dublin Society at Ballsbridge. From every point of view charming pictures met the eye — youth and beauty, fashion and elegance. It was par excellence the ladies' day, and dull sombre clad man may be pardoned if his looks of admiration were frequently prolonged. Many of the dresses worn by the fair sex were remarkable, if not daring in their originality, while others were beautiful examples of skill and taste, and infinite in their variety.' The Horse Show was generally thought to have been the best in its history.

While the Horse Show itself was hardly touched by the trouble in the city, as the weeks went by the effects of the lock-out were to spread to all classes in Dublin. To the wealthier people, though, it was not a matter of life and death but simply a troublesome nuisance. In September the society magazine, *Irish Life*, commented on the state of affairs in Dublin: 'As the industrial atmosphere has approached fever heat, the social barometer has fallen to zero; Dublin is plumbing the lowest depths of the dead season. There is literally nothing of interest to chronicle and the next few weeks do not offer any exciting engagements. The polo season is over, the cricket grounds are closed, the Phoenix Park has assumed its late autumn appearance; no flag flutters above the Vice-regal Lodge, which is closed for the present, the Lord Lieutenant and the Countess of Aberdeen having gone to Scotland...'

Things were to get even worse. The lock-out began to make life in the city very unpleasant, even for those not directly involved. With a touch of bitterness, the *Irish Life* magazine complained in October, that.... 'Any number of distinguished people have passed through Dublin during the past ten days. Small blame to them that they showed no inclination to tarry in the city, where the inconvenience caused by the strike is making itself unpleasantly felt in many ways'.

Dublin was an unhappy city.

PUBLIC OPINION

As the lock-out went on, everybody was forced to take sides in the dispute. There were very few people in the centre-ground, seeing merit in both the employers' and the workers' point of view. Typical of the thinking of a large section of the middle class was this imaginary dialogue which appeared in the *Irish Life* magazine in September: the two characters are talking in particular about the events of "Bloody Sunday", the day of the

86

Irreconcilable

It's a wrong thing to crush the workers,
It's a wrong thing to crush the workers;
It's a right thing to wipe out tyrants,
Fight on Transport Workers, prove that you are true
To Jim, the trusted leader, and the Red Hand Abu.

Heiton's Coal being delivered under police escort in O'Connell Street.

riots after Larkin's meeting.

'First person: I saw all that business in Sackville Street when Larkin was arrested, and it struck me that the police were severe but wisely so. An ugly riot was threatened and, if it had not been nipped in the bud, there would have been some rifle shooting on the part of the soldiers. People can never see that prevention is better than the cure. No one can deny that the police severity put a very quick end to rioting that would have continued for days if treated with a velvet glove.

'Second person: Quite so. There are in Dublin some thousands of gaol-birds who do not love the police. These fellows wait for the opportunity to have a fling at the police. The ordinary honest striker is seldom a rioter, he is only an excuse for hooliganism.'

Many people felt some sympathy for the strikers, but felt that the workers were being misled and that their tactics were wrong. The workers who refused to obey Larkin's orders to strike were praised by many others who admired their courage in standing up to the jibes of their striking colleagues.

Two letters to *The Irish Times*, within a few days of each other, summed up the arguments for and against Larkin's actions.

from Thomas J. Westropp, August 30th, 1913:

'Please receive £2 for the loyal men who are working the Tramways with grave personal risk and molestation. I hope the visitors to the Horse Show will take the opportunity of marking their appreciation of these men and their detestation of the extreme meddlers who kindled the disturbance at this time. The citizens should equally support the fund. It is our city that must ultimately suffer. That one of the few opportunities for its prosperity was not wrecked this year is owing largely to the tramwaymen who stuck to their duty.'

From E. A. Aston, Wednesday 3rd September, 1913:

'Twenty thousand families — one third of the people of Dublin — live in one room tenements. How many of our federated employers after twelve months of life under such conditions would think of abstract considerations of citizenship or industrial prosperity? Are they sure that their children would not learn to throw bottles at the police if society had condemned them to the reeking nursery of the tenement house.'

The newspapers that reported the events were nearly all

opposed to the methods of the strikers. Naturally, William Martin Murphy's newspaper was the most strongly opposed. On the first of September, the leading article of the *Irish Independent* described the happenings in the city: 'Out from the reeking slums, the jailbirds and the most abandoned creatures of both sexes have poured to vent their hatred upon their natural enemies, the police.'

The other newspapers, while not using such strong language, also criticised the strikers. Support for the workers came only in some articles written for small magazines and newspapers and, of course in the newspaper edited by Larkin himself, the *Irish Worker.*

Violence was common in the streets and after meetings. Jim Phelan, a young man at the time, remembers how workers caught up in the strike used to prepare themselves for the worst:

"At Inchicore, for instance, a couple of thousand men were employed, a large proportion living in Dublin. Since tramway work was a blackleg activity, and since travelling in trams carried a stigma, these hundreds made the long trail to and from the city each morning and evening on foot...

Typical dialogue between two law-abiding citizens of the time, neither perhaps an ardent sympathiser with the Labour cause; to a smith at Inchicore works, a friend might approach towards evening for a gossip:

'Looks like rain, Mick.'

'Aye' — (pause) — 'I wish the bloody strike was over, that a man didn't have to thramp the streets into Dublin, and could ride the bloody tram, ordinary.'

'Aye, indeed. A lousy road, into the city, on a wet night especial.' (pause). 'There's a meeting at Inchicore Cross just after knock-off time.'

'Oh! Should be good. They say that big Daly fella's a fine speaker. If it's not too wet —'

'Me too — they say Jim Larkin'll be out here himself speakin' tonight.'

'Uh - huh. *That'll* be broke up of course' — (pause) — 'There's no way of gettin' past the bloody polis at Inchicore Cross. That means the long way round for anyone who wants to miss the meetin'.'

'Uh - huh. An' I hate that bloody road, on a wet night.'

'Me, too.' (pause) 'To hell with them. I'm going by Inchicore Cross.'

'Sure, sure.' (more briskly). 'You'll be shoeing a shaft, then?'
'Aye.'
'Make it two.'

Shoeing a shaft was simple but uneconomic and illegal. It consisted of selecting a new sledge-hammer handle, a piece of hickory about four feet long, shaped to the hand and thickened at one end. A short piece of iron piping was made red-hot, slid on to the thick end of the hammer-shaft and water-cooled into position. Equipped with two of these, the pair of citizens could start on foot for their distant homes, might even risk paying a call at the Labour meeting en route to hear the fiery, world-famous orator Jim Larkin. Since a shod-shaft was a foot longer and a pound heavier than a constabulary baton, the Inchicore worthies often reached home almost undamaged."

"THE HIGHEST POINT OF MORAL GRANDEUR"

At the start of September, the British Trade Unions held a congress in Manchester. Three delegates from Dublin attended. and the Congress, hearing their report, promised the support of the British unions to their colleagues in Dublin. They undertook to provide food for the starving families of the striking Dublin workers. A British union delegation travelled to Dublin to try to bring about a settlement. After meeting representatives of the employers, they returned home having made no progress.

The situation in Dublin was getting desperate: starvation was widespread in the tenements. Then on Saturday 28th September a ship, "The Hare", arrived in Dublin carrying food gathered by British trade unionists. On board the ship were 60,000 "family boxes", each box holding enough food for five people. Thousands of people lined up at Liberty Hall, holding vouchers ready to be exchanged for their boxes. The food-ship had a great effect on the morale of the strikers. It showed them that the workers of Britain supported them in their struggle. Food kitchens were set up in Liberty Hall, and after all the British family boxes had been given out, bread and soup became the usual menu for the starving Dubliners.

James Larkin had been in jail since Bloody Sunday. On his release on bail from Mountjoy Prison, he went to England in order to gain as much support there as possible. Speaking to huge meetings, he got a great response from English workers: sympathetic strikes continued in Manchester, Liverpool and Birmingham.

A drawing of a food kitchen in Liberty Hall by Sir William Orpen who was involved in the "Save the Kiddies Campaign".

BRITISH TRADES UNION CONGRESS & DUBLIN TRADES COUNCIL.

BRITISH TRADE UNION FUND.

Give Bearer Parcel Bread, &c.

Apply—South Wall. From 12 noon to 6 p.m. Saturday, 27th Sept., 1913.

J. A. SEDDIN,
T. MacPARTLIN.

O'KEEFFE, Trade Union Printer, 8 Halston St., Dublin.

A voucher for a food parcel.

Larkin and Connolly attempted to push the British trade unions into a general stoppage of work in support of the Dublin workers. The leaders of the unions, however, were not prepared to go that far. This failure was something which Larkin and Connolly never forgave, and left them bitterly disappointed.

Back in Dublin, many attempts were being made to bring about a settlement of the dispute. A Peace Commission headed by Professor Thomas Kettle failed to achieve anything. Sir George Askwith was appointed to lead a special commission by the British Government. This commission produced a report which was balanced: it criticised the unions for the use of the sympathetic strike, but also said that the document drawn up by the employers, outlawing the Irish Transport and General Workers Union, 'would force people to work under conditions which no workman or body of workmen could reasonably be expected to accept.' The employers replied to the commission, saying that they could not accept the proposals of the commission. "Larkinism" had to be crushed, once and for all. They claimed that, though they favoured the principle of trade unionism, they could not accept the Larkin style of operation. Their lawyer summed up their attitude when he first addressed the commission: 'Trade Unionism in the mouths of these people (Larkin and his comrades) is a mockery; it exists only in name. The men are puppets in the hands of three or four of the leaders. Mr. Larkin acts the part of a Napoleon; he orders this or that, and the men obey him, and that is what brought about the strikes.' There could be no peace, said the employers, until Larkinism was dead. Though the workers were willing to enter talks, the employers refused. So the agony of Dublin continued.

Around this time, a leading Irish writer, George Russell (who signed himself 'AE') wrote a letter to the newspapers in which he addressed "the masters of Dublin".

'It remained for the twentieth century and the capital city of Ireland to see four hundred masters deciding openly upon starving one hundred thousand people, and refusing to consider any solution except that fixed by their pride. You, masters, asked men to do that which masters of labour in any other city in these islands had not dared to do. You insolently demanded of those men who were members of a trade union that they should resign from that union: and from those who were not members you insisted on a vow that they would never join it.

'You may succeed in your policy and ensure your own

92

A crowd of workers waiting for the first food ship from Britain
Saturday 28 September 1913.

THE IRISH WORKER — 1911 — June 10th

Irreconcilable

They will not let my Daddy work —
that's what my mammy said.
Then how am I to get my milk
— or Mammy get the bread?
Must I in vain with hunger cry
and famish too with cold?
Is it with little children's tears
that rich men make their gold?

damnation by your victory. The men whose manhood you have broken will loathe you, and will always be brooding and scheming to strike a fresh blow. The children will be taught to curse you. The infant being moulded in the womb will have breathed into its starved body the vitality of hate. It is not they — it is you who are blind Samsons pulling down the pillars of the social order.' (Dublin, October 6th, 1913.)

This letter had a deep effect on many of those who read it. Many other writers and thinkers of the time came out publicly in support of the workers. Not all went as far as 'AE'. Some who were sympathetic to the workers, also thought that the employers had a just cause as well. The young Professor Tom Kettle, wrote: 'The ordinary employer is neither so big nor so bad as he appears in AE's stormy vision.'

"SAVE THE KIDDIES"

As the dispute dragged through October, it became clear that not even the food kitchens of Liberty Hall would be enough to keep starvation from running riot in the city. A plan was proposed by some women to send children of the strikers to homes in England, where they could be adequately cared for by families there. The idea appealed to Larkin because it was so daring and he set about organising it. The plan, however, raised the disapproval of the Church. The Archbishop of Dublin wrote to the newspapers:

Archbishop's House,
Dublin.
20th October, 1913.

Dear Sir — I have read with nothing short of consternation in some of our evening newspapers that a movement is on foot, and has already made some progress, to induce the wives of the working men who are now unemployed by reason of the present deplorable industrial deadlock in Dublin, to hand over their children to be cared for in England by persons of whom they, of course, can have no knowledge whatever.

The Dublin women now subjected to this cruel temptation to part with their helpless offspring are, in the majority of cases, Catholics. Have they abandoned their Faith? Surely not. Well, if they have not, they should need no words of mine to remind them of the plain duty of every Catholic mother in such a case. I can only put it to them that they can be no longer held worthy of the name of Catholic mothers if they so far forget that duty as to

94

Top - 'The Hare' a food ship from Britain arrives in Dublin.

Left - Larkin watches from the Quays.

send away their little children to be cared for in a strange land, without security of any kind that those to whom the poor children are to be handed over are Catholics, or indeed are persons of any faith at all.

I am much mistaken if this recent and most mischievous development of our labour trouble in Dublin fails to appeal to all who are involved in the conflict, employers or employed as they may be, or fails to move them to strive with all earnestness to bring the conflict to an end.

WILLIAM J. WALSH,
Archbishop of Dublin

Violent scenes occurred as parents brought their children to the docks to send them across to England. Groups organised by Catholic parents and priests blocked the way to the ships, and scuffles broke out between the two parties. More than any other event in the course of the three-month old dispute, the sending away of the children raised the wildest emotions in people. James Connolly replied to the Archbishop, on behalf of the I.T.G.W.U.: 'Nobody wants to send the children away — the Irish Transport and General Workers Union least of all desires such a sacrifice. But neither do we wish the children to starve.' The plan had aroused too much anger for it to succeed, and was therefore dropped. The children were to remain on in Dublin, and manage as best they could.

The Chief Secretary, Augustine Birrell, reported on the affair to the Prime Minister: 'It certainly was an outrage. For in the first place, there are no starving children in Dublin, and in the second place, the place swarms with homes for them. It was a new advertising dodge of a few silly women, but it has broken the strike.' Birrell's report was not true on a number of counts, but the "save-the-kiddies" campaign as it was known, undoubtedly turned a great deal of public sympathy away from the workers.

Sir William Orpen describes an incident during the "save the kiddies' campaign:

'One afternoon Professor Sheehy Skeffington was to take two children to the Kingsbridge Station and hand them over to Lady X, who was going to keep them at her place in Meath. The professor did not turn up in time, and Larkin said, "Orpen, would you be good enough to take them?" "Certainly," said I, and went off downstairs with the two poor little things. About half-way down I met the professor hurrying up. "What are you doing with these children?" said he. I explained that as he was not there,

Larkin had asked me to see them to Kingsbridge. "This is my business," said the professor, and held out his hand to the children, and went on downstairs. So I returned to Jim, told him what had happened, and took my place to watch and wonder at the strange things to be seen in that dirty room, which was on the second storey. But even there the air was pungent with the smell of the cauldrons of soup from the basement, and of the Dubliners who came with their bottles, tin cans, or any kind of utensil that would hold this hot, life-giving stuff. All day long lines of starving people waiting for their turn, very quiet and silent, no rough words or jostling; they were too weak for such things. It was a sad sight. Suddenly we heard great noises and loud words. The door burst open, and in came a lot of people with Sheehy Skeffington. He had nothing on except a blanket wrapped around him. When he was delivering the children to Lady X at Kingsbridge, the anti-Larkinites attacked him and tore all his clothes off. I nearly got that.'

"THE FIERY CROSS"

James Larkin was sentenced to seven months imprisonment for incitement, on October 28th. In his absence the workers were led by James Connolly and his other close colleagues. However, such was the pressure on the government, that Larkin was released on November 13th. He immediately left on another tour of England, drumming up support for the stricken city of Dublin. His reception was huge. "The Fiery Cross" campaign, as he referred to his series of torch-lit meetings, caught the imagination of the British workers. The Irish Labour leaders still aimed to get the British unions to come out in a general sympathetic strike, but despite Larkin's great reception, the union leaders in England were not prepared to take this final step.

By Christmas 1913, the outlook for the jobless Dublin workers was extremely bleak. The food ships from England, their life-line, could no longer be depended upon. 'It may well be,' wrote Tom Kettle, 'that the critical moment has come. There is a limit to human endurance, and a point beyond which the belt cannot be tightened.'

The choice was gradually becoming more and more clear to each worker — surrender or starve. William Martin Murphy, in the early days of what he had imagined would be a very short dispute had said: 'The employer all the time managed to get his

Irish Citizen Army parading outside Liberty Hall.

three meals a day, but the unfortunate workman and his family had no resources whatever except submission, and that was what occurred in 99 cases out of a 100. The difficulty in teaching that lesson to the workmen was extraordinary.' Murphy was then speaking in September: he thought he was speaking at the end of the affair. The workers, in fact, stayed out for a further six months, without their "three meals a day". They could not stay out for ever.

THE IRISH CITIZEN ARMY

The violence used by police against workers caused great resentment. In a number of speeches, James Larkin had hinted that he favoured the idea of the workers organising themselves into a defensive force. This idea appealed to a number of people, who began discussing its possibilities. In October 1913, Captain Jack White, who had already been involved in the lock-out, approached Larkin with a definite plan to set up such a force. Enthusiastically, Larkin seized on the idea. At one of the regular mass-meetings held outside Liberty Hall, he announced the plan to the assembled crowd: 'Labour in its own defence must begin to train itself to act with disciplined courage and with organised and concentrated force...'

Captain White, who had a distinguished military record, took command of the newly formed Irish Citizen Army. He organised regular military training sessions, and demanded full commitment and rigid discipline. The standards that Captain White achieved were not always as high as he wished. Many volunteers in the army found that the training was too severe: attendances fell at the weekly sessions. Often Larkin or Connolly would call meetings at a time when White was holding a training session. At such times, military activities were hopeless. Despite these difficulties, the Irish Citizen Army survived and grew. It was not called into much direct action in the course of the rest of the lock-out. However, even after the end of the dispute, the Citizen Army continued to drill. Under the very able leadership of White, Sean O'Casey, Constance Markievicz, Francis Sheehy-Skeffington and others, the Citizen Army became a permanent symbol of the Labour movement's strength. By 1916, under the guidance of James Connolly, they were planning an insurrection against the government.

"SINN FÉIN" AND LABOUR

With the outbreak of the Great War, "Sinn Féin" activity grew rapidly. After the events of 1916, the Sinn Féin Party became much stronger and by 1918 had taken over from the Home Rule Party, as by far the largest party in Ireland. Arthur Griffith, the founder of the party, had always stressed the importance of breaking the link with England. 'The most important lesson for the Irish people to thoroughly learn is that whether the English call themselves Liberals or Tories, Imperialists or Socialists — they are always the English', he wrote as far back as 1904. On this point he came into strong disagreement with Larkin and the other leaders of the labour movement, who saw no difference between English and Irish bosses.

The dislike that grew between Larkin and Griffith was almost as big as that between Larkin and Murphy. Griffith frequently attacked Larkin, calling him a "strike organiser", and "the representative of English trades-unionism in Ireland". When the lock-out occurred in 1913, Griffith showed little sympathy for the workers. The food-ships from England he saw as a dangerous bribe. Similarly, when the "save-the-kiddies" campaign began he was strongly opposed: 'The number of Dublin parents who would consent to send their children to be nurtured in the homes of the enemies of their race do not form five per cent of the parents affected by the strike.'

Not all of Griffith's supporters shared his opinion of Larkin and his union. Radical, and mainly young, members of Sinn Féin supported the strikers, to some extent. People like Eamon Ceannt had come to admire much of what the labour leaders had achieved. In the newspaper *Irish Freedom,* they put their case: 'The Masters of Dublin went too far when they declared war on the men's organisations, and even the lowest strata of industrial society took up the gauntlets with a promptitude and courage worthy of their race... The employers are not to be blamed overmuch for they also are so involved in the system that only minor changes are within their power, be they ever so willing.' This was the position of most republicans of the time — favouring the workers, but with some reservations. Padraig Pearse put it like this 'I do not know whether the methods of Mr. James Larkin are wise methods or unwise methods (unwise I think in some respects), but this I know, that here is a most hideous wrong to be righted, and the man who attempts honestly to right it is a good man and a brave man.'

After 1913, Connolly worked closely with the 'republican' wing of Sinn Féin, led by people like Thomas Clarke and Pearse. They persuaded him to join with them in the rising of 1916 — Connolly had planned on leading the Citizen Army on his own. In the years after Connolly's death in 1916, however, the influence of Labour leaders on Sinn Féin was to grow much less.

*Trams were a popular and **effective** means of advertising, **as** can be
seen in this photograph. This view shows O'Connell Bridge
and Burgh Quay from Bachelors' Walk.*

7
Back to Work

If there is peace in Dublin it is not that of a healthy civilisation.
— Thomas Kettle

WITH THE FAILURE of the British Trade Unions to come out in sympathetic strike, the cause of the Dublin workers was doomed. Supplies of money and food from Britain dwindled away and the strikers had to face the prospect of returning to work. On January 18th, 1914 leaders of the I.T.G.W.U. met secretly. They advised their members to return to work, if they could do so without signing the hated employers' document. Many were able to do this but some employers still refused to take back workers who did not sign the document. In a speech on January 30th, Larkin publicly declared: 'We are beaten. We make no bones about it; but we are not too badly beaten still to fight.'

Two days later, the Builders Labourers Union — about 3,000 men — surrendered to the employers and signed the documents promising never to join the I.T.G.W.U. This was the turning point: the strike was then seen to be over and other workers in the city slowly drifted back to work on the employers' terms. In February, 1914, James Connolly wrote with great bitterness: 'And so we Irish workers must go down into Hell, bow our backs to the lash of the slave driver.... and eat the dust of defeat and betrayal.'

The defeat of the workers left their leaders very disappointed. Larkin and Connolly now directed their anger not at the employers of Dublin but at the leaders of the British trade unions who refused to come out on strike in support of their colleagues in Dublin. As the months went by however, it became clear that the employers had not won a total victory. Workers who had

*Trinity College, Dublin, at five-to-one on a sunny day. Men appear
to be painting the railings, at the front gate.*

promised never to join the I.T.G.W.U. slowly began to drift back into the union. Within a short time, the I.T.G.W.U. was once more the largest union in the city. No employer was willing to sack large numbers of his workforce who had rejoined the union: a second lock-out was as frightening to the employers as it was to the workers.

In June 1914, all the Irish trade unions came together for their annual congress. Larkin gave a long speech to the delegates there, and he referred to the events of the previous year in a proud manner: 'The lock-out in 1913 was a deliberate attempt to starve us into submission and met with well-deserved failure... The employers claim a victory but the employers did not beat back organised labour in this city. I admit we had to retreat to base, but that was owing to the treachery of leaders in affiliated unions and betrayal in our own ranks.'

William Martin Murphy and the employers did indeed claim a victory. They believed that Larkinism had been decisively defeated at last. Now, they hoped, things could return to the way they had been before Larkin's arrival in Dublin. *The Irish Times* newspaper saw the position somewhat more clearly than did the employers. A leading article in the paper declared: 'The very necessary business of "smashing Larkin" is successfully accomplished; but that is very far from being the same thing as "smashing Larkinism". There is no security whatever that the men who are now going about their work brooding over the bitterness of defeat will not endeavour to re-organise their broken forces and, given another leader and another opportunity, strike a further and a more desperate blow at the economic life of Dublin.' Though the city was at peace once again, a sense of unease was common. The lock-out and strike had really decided nothing: future relations between employers and workers remained unclear.

Looking back over the whole episode in November 1914, James Connolly wrote: 'The battle was a drawn battle. The employers were unable to carry on their business without men and women who remained loyal to their union. The workers were unable to force their employers to a formal recognition of the union and to give preference to organised labour. From the effects of this drawn battle both sides are still bearing scars. How deep these scars are none will reveal.'

Aside from the scars borne by both sides, one of the effects of the dispute was to make people more aware of the urgent need to improve living conditions in Dublin. Prompted by Lady

Aberdeen, a Civic Exhibition was held in July 1914. Among the most important items of the Exhibition were a section on town-planning and a competition for a 'Dublin Development Scheme'. These were now vitally important issues, of concern to all.

The Civic Exhibition held in Dublin in July 1914, was intended to be a memorable event in the history of the city. The outbreak of the Great War in Europe, however, intervened and the importance of the exhibition was lost.

8
The Aftermath of Dublin, 1913

Inscription for a Headstone — Austin Clarke

What Larkin bawled to hungry crowds
Is murmured now in dining-hall
And study — Faith bestirs itself
Lest infidels in their impatience
Leave it behind. Who could have guessed
Batons were blessings in disguise,
When every ambulance was filled
With half-killed men and Sunday trampled
Upon unrest. Such fear can harden
Or soften heart, knowing too clearly
His name endures on our holiest page
Scrawled in a rage by Dublin's poor.

THE PRINCIPAL FIGURES of the events in Dublin in 1913 — William Martin Murphy and James Larkin — never again reached the same degree of public influence. Murphy died in Dublin 1919, a rich, powerful and well-respected man of 73 years. After the exciting events of 1913 he retreated from public life, spending his last years in semi-retirement. On his death, he left an estate of over a quarter-million pounds. Larkin left Ireland for a tour of America at the end of 1914. The trip was part holiday and part work, as he was to lecture and collect support for the I.T.G.W.U. from friendly sources in America. True to his character, Larkin found himself involved in trouble while in America, being imprisoned for incitement to riot. He did not return to Ireland until 1923.

Though the main characters faded quickly from the public eye, the effects of the events in Dublin were many and long-

A busy scene on Grafton Street, the fashionable shopping-centre of the city. "Sandwich-men" carry billboards advertising the Trocadero Restaurant, while a jarvey in the foreground carries a bicycle on the roof as it heads up towards St. Stephen's Green.

lasting. The social conditions which were the first cause of the troubles were now seen by everybody. It was agreed by all that they could no longer be tolerated. The sacrifices of the thousands of poor Dublin families during the lock-out slowly began to pay off, as more attention was paid to improving housing, health and sanitary conditions in the city. The situation did not improve overnight, but it was clear that radical changes would have to be made if further trouble was to be avoided. No longer could the wealthy classes ignore the poverty of their own city. The trade union movement was now firmly established, with the I.T.G.W.U. as the major union in the country. When Larkin left for America, he appointed James Connolly to take charge in his absence. Connolly became particularly interested in the Citizen Army and found himself also attracted to certain elements within Sinn Féin and the Irish Republican Brotherhood.

The lock-out of 1913 was the first in a series of events which were to change Irish life drastically. In 1914, the Great War broke out in Europe. Ireland as part of the United Kingdom was brought into this and many Irishmen went off to fight in the battlefields of Europe. James Connolly and Republicans such as Padraig Pearse, Sean MacDiarmuida and others opposed any Irish involvement in "Britain's war". They planned for an armed rising against British forces in Ireland. So it was that the Citizen Army, founded in the heat of the 1913 struggle, was led by Connolly to join a group of Irish volunteers led by Pearse and others in an insurrection at Easter 1916. The failure of the rising, and the execution of Connolly, Pearse and the others was the start of the campaign which eventually led to the setting-up of the Irish Free State in 1921 and a new chapter in Irish history. Sinn Féin — the small party of years before — had by then become the most powerful political party in the country and the Home Rule Movement was well and truly dead.

When James Larkin returned to Ireland from America in 1923, he found a country very different from the one he had left. It was not to his liking, however. He disagreed with Connolly's participation in the 1916 rising and was shocked that the party of his old enemy, Arthur Griffith, should now hold power in Ireland. Larkin thought the achievements of the 1913 struggle had been lost in the smoke of the fight for independence. He found himself in disagreement with his old colleagues in the I.T.G.W.U., and founded a new union, the Workers Union of Ireland. For the rest of his life he remained dissatisfied with his country, and when he died in 1947 he died a disappointed man.

There was much truth in Larkin's view, but he was too severe in his judgements. For the great upheaval in Dublin in 1913 had without doubt started a process which brought about great changes in the living standards of the poor. An American historian, J. D. Clarkson, later wrote: 'In the deepest sense, "Larkinism" had triumphed. The Dublin struggle had fired the hearts and minds of the working classes throughout the length and breadth of Ireland... Most significant of all, the most helpless of all classes had learned the lesson of its power and in the learning had proved itself worthy of Ireland's bravest traditions.'

Through the sufferings of the workers of Dublin, the Irish Labour Movement had come of age. The dispute of 1913 remains unique in Irish history, a monument of social agony and courage.

Church Street, Dublin 1913.

Index

ACKNOWLEDGEMENTS

We would like to thank Dermot Stokes and Simon Hewat, for work in the development of the materials; Mary Daly and Frank O'Connor for suggestions during the preparation of the collection; Professor Louis Cullen and Donal Nevin for reading and commenting on an earlier version of the manuscript.

ILLUSTRATION ACKNOWLEDGEMENTS

The publishers would like to thank and acknowledge the following for permission to reproduce photographs or documents: The Lawrence Collection (at the National Library of Ireland), pages 6, 9, 11, 15, 21 (bottom), 25 (bottom), 27, 33, 65, 101, 103, 107; The Guinness Museum, pages 21 (top), 48 (by kind permission of Dr. H. S. Corran), 57; Dublin Corporation, pages 29, 41, 46, 52, 55, 109; The Royal Society of Antiquaries of Ireland, pages 35, 37, 39, 43, 49, 59. We also thank F. E. Dixon for supplying the illustrations for pages 13 (top), 17, 25 (top) and 105. The illustrations which appear on pages 13 (bottom), 31, 67, 71, 83, 85, 87, 93 and 95 (top) are reproduced from *Irish Life* magazine. Illustrations reproduced from *Fifty Years of Liberty Hall,* published by the I.T.G.W.U., appear on pages 79, 91 and 98. Illustrations reproduced from *1913 Jim Larkin and the Dublin Lock-Out,* published by the Workers Union of Ireland, appear on pages 63 and 70.

We gratefully acknowledge permission to use copyright material in this book: to Mr. James Plunkett for extracts from his play *Big Jim* and from *Strumpet City,* Hutchinson; to the Executors of the Joyce Estate for extracts from *Dubliners* published by Jonathan Cape Ltd.; to the Editor, *Dublin Historical Record* for extracts from Vol.30, No.4 "My Dublin" by Moira Lysaght; to Mr. Sean O'Faolain for quote from "Portrait of the Artist as an Old Man", *Irish University Review,* Spring 1976. The quotations by Sean O'Casey are from *Drums under the Window,* Macmillan & Co.; by E. O'Malley are from *On Another Man's Wounds*; by Jim Phelan are from *The First Part of the Autobiography* Sedwidge & Jackson. In instances where we have been unable to contact copyright owners, we would appreciate their writing to the publisher.